PORTRAIT OF A HOLOCAUST CHILD

Memories and Reflections

PORTRAIT OF A HOLOCAUST CHILD

Memories and Reflections

RITA KASIMOW BROWN

This book was published with the support of:

 Yad Vashem
The Holocaust Martyrs' and Heroes' Remembrance Authority
The Foundation for Support of Survivors' Memoirs

 The Azrieli Group

 **The Azrieli Foundation**

 The Jehoshua Rabinovich Tel Aviv Foundation for the Arts

The design, data and editing of this publication are the responsibility of the author.

Copyright © Rita Kasimow Brown
Jerusalem 2010/5770

All rights reserved. No part of this publication may be translated, reproduced, stored in a retrieval system or transmitted, in any form or by any means, electronic, mechanical, photocopying, recording or otherwise, without express written permission from the publishers.

Cover Painting by Rita Kasimow Brown
Prepared for print by Stephane Zerbib, Photographer
Cover and Typesetting by S. Kim Glassman

ISBN: 978-965-229-482-1

1 3 5 7 9 8 6 4 2

Gefen Publishing House, Ltd.
6 Hatzvi Street
Jerusalem 94386, Israel
972-2-538-0247
orders@gefenpublishing.com

Gefen Books
600 Broadway
Lynbrook, NY 11563, USA
1-800-477-5257
orders@gefenpublishing.com

www.gefenpublishing.com

Printed in Israel   *Send for our free catalogue*

To my son Alan and my daughter Deenah. Thank you for the love and support during the episodes of chaos in my life. You were and are my light in the tunnel forever.

I'm grateful to my daughter-in-law Yael, who supported me in many ways, especially in my art projects. And I'm filled with gratitude to my brother, Professor Harold Kasimow, who believed in me, encouraged me and gave me a generous donation which made it possible to publish this book.

I also dedicate this book to Yasmin, Gideon, and Yair, my wonderful, loving and beautiful grandchildren. You have brought joy and hope into my life.

CONTENTS

Preface ix
Introduction xi
   Historical Background.. xiii
Prologue... xv

DIARY EXCERPTS
   Awake..3
   Childhood in Turmont..5
   The Coming of the Nazis 8
   Correspondence with "Jay" 18
   The "Grub"..22
   We Leave the Grub 42
   The March to Freedom 47
   Home Sweet Home...57

Epilogue
   A Dream: A Dialogue with Jay 71
   Muddy Waters..77

Bibliography 79

Selected paintings by the author 49

PREFACE

The book *Portrait of a Holocaust Child* is based on parts of my diary. It illustrates episodes from the period of my Holocaust experience and exposes its influence on my life. The book also contains paintings and descriptions of my dreams, giving profound expression to my mental survival. I survived thanks to my art and creativity, and the heroism of my parents who risked their lives every minute of every day to save their children.

In the spring of 2006 I went to Poland for a visit and to participate in the March of the Living in Auschwitz. The questions crossing my mind addressed the issue of whether art can save us from the awful memories of the past, from the horrific valley of the dead that Birkenau-Auschwitz has come to represent in the Jewish psyche as well as throughout most of the world – the epitome of barbarianism committed by human against human. While it is easier to think that the horrors of the Holocaust were committed by German "animals" or "demons," we must never forget that these horrors were actually perpetrated by human beings. Can my faith in humanity be restored? Can I avert my eyes from death and destruction? Will I have the courage to create?

I do believe that art and the imagination can heal the soul and enrich it. My visit to Poland enabled me to shed the images of death and to embrace the "shadow" within me. Thus triumphant, I can now continue with my art and my creative efforts.

Almost miraculously did pain turn into images and ambivalence into shape and color – a kind of wonderful chemical process in which creating art nourishes one's inner self, linking one's conscious self with feelings and thoughts of the unconscious.

I survived the Nazi murder machine, determined to have the courage and will to be creative. This paved the way for two exhibitions over the last three years.

I went through many hardships to publish this book. I have had many disappointments and discouragements. Some individuals who promised to help me did not come through and one individual took money from me and did not edit the book as he had promised. Whenever I fall in my life, there comes an angel or angels that pick me up out of my "hole." The last two angels are Professor Margo Schotz and her husband Amiel Schotz. I am grateful for their input into the book and for their part in restoring my faith in human beings.

I am grateful to my longtime friend Mrs. Golda Och and her husband Dr. Michael Och, who encouraged me in my project and contributed a generous donation to this book, believing in the book's important addition to the Holocaust memorial. Mrs. Golda Och and I were close friends throughout our student years at Columbia University and the Jewish Theological Seminary of New York, and we have remained friends until today.

I thank Professor Emeritus Iran Sever, who has followed my career and given me very helpful advice during my many uncertainties throughout the project.

I am grateful to Rina Rosler, my very devoted friend who has listened for endless hours to my woes and has given me positive encouragement in all my ups and downs for many years.

I would also like to thank Roberto Basham, a volunteer sent by the Amcha organization, who for the last few months has been helping me and standing by me through the last pains of giving birth to this book.

I can be contacted at bkasimow@gmail.com. My art can be viewed at the Urban Gallery site, or on my site: http://sites.google.com/site/kasimowbrownrita/Home.

INTRODUCTION

I was born in Poland, in the town of Turmont, where I lived with my family. When the Nazis started persecuting the Jews in my town, my family and others spent many months in the small ghetto of Dryswiaty, Belarus, doing forced labor. My family – that is my parents, my two siblings and myself – managed to escape, thus beginning our odyssey, wandering from place to place, hiding in barns, cattle sheds, pigsties, grottos and caves in the forests until we buried ourselves alive in a tomb, a hole in the ground on a distant farm called Malaki. There we stayed hidden for twenty months, almost unable to move our limbs, hungry, surrounded by total silence, suffocating in the darkness – in short, more dead than alive. This lasted until 1945 when the army of the USSR drove the Germans out of Poland. After our liberation we were taken to a displaced persons camp in Bad Reichenhall, Germany. In 1949 we immigrated to the USA, where I finished high school and earned several academic degrees.

In 1971 I made aliyah with my two children. My three grandchildren were born in Israel. Thus my wanderings came to an end.

I am a psychologist, art therapist, and artist. Imagination and creativity have saved my life. In 1995, I participated in a summer program of art and movement therapy at Lesley College in Boston. The course prompted me to review my life, from childhood until now. In one exercise, we were to imagine ourselves at the age of sixty-five. I had the opportunity to carry on a dialogue with my future self. At the end of the workshop, I expressed the wish to be a narrator of my life, to step back from the chaos and make sense of it spiritually.

In 1998, I began to feel an urgent desire to record my Holocaust memories, so I began writing a diary in which I have reflected upon how my experiences in the Holocaust have influenced my life. I don't want to die, taking my extremely painful, yet valuable, experiences with me without leaving a memorial. As with all Holocaust survivors, I am aging, and feel that my time may be running out. The recent Intifadas have only served to increase my sense of urgency.

In addition to recording my daily life and memories, I have also included accounts of some of my dreams, as well as dialogues with dream figures, using Carl Jung's method called "active imagination." In Jung's words, active imagination is "a sequence of fantasies produced by deliberation and concentration" on a particular image. A "healing of the imagination by the imagination," this "inner dialogue" involves producing images, concentrating on them, associating, integrating, and exploring the imagination. According to Jung, trying to integrate one's "self" with the "shadow" that lies within is what gives meaning to our lives. Shut out that shadow and life loses its meaning. Thus, self and shadow complement one another, with the shadow enabling one to reach the light. James Hillman, in his book *Dreams and the Underworld*, maintains that in our daily experiences and dreams we feel both Heaven and Hell. He further explains that the highest level of creativity contains both our inner Paradise and Hell as one entity.

Jungian depth psychology adds a larger dimension to people's struggles for growth, awareness of polarities, and complexities of the human psyche. Active imagination is not a passive fantasy; it is experiential and offers us insight into our inner worlds. Painting can be another mode to express active imagination; the painting on this book's cover, entitled *Figments of Imagination*, was inspired through active imagination. Western culture's emphasis on the rational, technological, and biochemical aspects of the human mind have been deeply changed by Jung's theories, which focus on the emotional, esoteric, and psychosocial side of life.

Dreams, and how they affect my conscious and unconscious life have been an important factor in understanding myself and reaching a higher level of consciousness. It seems to be a kind of search for the meaning of life, which I must admit, has eluded me until now. Who am I? What is my life all about? Is life an illusion? What is reality and what is a dream? When I was a child in the Holocaust, the dream was my reality and reality was a nightmare.

HISTORICAL BACKGROUND

Rita Kasimow Brown, author of the book *Portrait of a Holocaust Child*, was born in the small town of Turmont, Poland. Turmont was established in 1789 as the private estate of a Russian scientist. During the nineteenth century it evolved into a community of about two hundred inhabitants, only a few of them Jewish. Turmont and Dryswiaty were located between Poland, Lithuania and Russia from 1914 to 1945. Rita's personal account, related in her book, cannot be properly appreciated without an understanding of Polish, Lithuanian and Russian history in the early twentieth century.

During the period of 1914–1945, the Polish and Lithuanian borders shifted many times, affecting the township of Turmont. Their history during the twentieth century was very tumultuous, involving many territorial changes resulting from two world wars as well as local wars.

Upon the outbreak of WWI in 1914, no Polish or Lithuanian States existed, as – owing to the spoils of war – their territories had been absorbed by the German, Austro-Hungarian, and Russian empires. This changed when the former two entered the Russian-held parts of Poland, Warsaw having been occupied in August 1915 and Vilna the following month. Thus, the issue of an independent state as well as political unity arose once again.

On November 5, 1916, the German government proclaimed the creation of a new, nominally independent Polish State. The Allied governments, for their part and in order to counter this move and gain Polish support for their cause, responded by promising the Poles independence once victory was achieved. Thus, with the Allied forces victorious, Poland became a sovereign state, whereas Lithuania and Belarus were absorbed into the Soviet Union. In consequence, Turmont in 1918–1919 reverted to Poland. However, Turmont having depended heavily on Zarasai in Lithuania, its economy started to decline and this, in turn, led to the dwindling of its population, who went looking for greener pastures. Even though the exact number of Turmont's inhabitants at that time is unknown, this exodus left only about three hundred inhabitants at the outbreak of WWII.

During the ensuing German occupation, a harsh policy of anti-Semitism and anti-communism was enforced and street violence against Jews and political dissenters was encouraged; in fact, actively promoted. For this purpose the occupation authorities made use of surviving ultra-nationalist elements from the pre-Soviet era in both Lithuania and Belarus by appointing them to official positions in local government. These officials took an active part in organizing massacres of the local Jews, in addition to the policy of gathering entire Jewish communities in ghettoes and concentration camps.

On August 26, 1941, local Lithuanian militias forcibly took a large number of the Turmont Jews to Deguciai Forest, where they were massacred.

The remnants were taken to the ghetto of Breslau, about fifteen miles east of Dryswiaty, thence to concentration camps.

So ended Jewish life in Turmont and Dryswiaty.[1]

---

1. The historical background is based on John Katz's unpublished article, "Turmont between Poland and Lithuania, 1914–1945."

PROLOGUE

In an interview conducted by Shmerke Kaczerginski in 1945, my parents Nachum Kasimow and Musia Levine recalled the destruction of the Jews in Turmont, Dryswiaty, and Widze. The interview was originally published in Yiddish in Kaczerginski's book, Hurban Vilne, *in the chapter entitled "The Destruction of Jews in Turmont, Dryswiaty, and Widze." The following is a verbatim translation of the original Yiddish.*

Until the war, we lived in Dryswiaty,[2] Belarus, 160 kilometers from Vilna. On July 2, 1941, the Germans invaded. On June 25, 1941, there had been a pogrom against the Jews.

Eighty-five Jews lived in Dryswiaty. Those responsible for the pogrom were mostly Lithuanians and a few Poles. During this pogrom, two Jews were shot dead: Isaac Volon (they had tortured him for two days prior to shooting him) and Shlomo Hammer.

A few days later the Germans invaded. They evacuated all the Jews (and did not let them take any possessions) across the border to Lithuanian territory (twelve kilometers from Turin) in the village of Driz. The Jews were in Driz for two weeks. During this time, twenty-four Poles were shot to death in Turmont.

After this incident, the Jews were returned to Dryswiaty and

---

2. Before the war, the family owned two homes – one in Dryswiaty and one in Turmont, where the family business was located. All the Kasimow children were born in Turmont.

lived there until the arrival of the Gestapo. They ordered us to make boots, dresses, and watches, and then left.

On Monday, March 23, the Gestapo invaded and decreed that all heads of household had to bring whatever goods they possessed. After they brought everything, they beat them ferociously and sent a wagon to every Jewish house to transport the Jews to the Widze ghetto. In Widze, they gathered other Jews from the nearby towns of Droysk, Opse, Dubnow and Kazan.

However, the Gestapo selected five Jewish families in Dryswiaty for skilled and hard labor. We were included among them.

Jews could not hide with peasants because many peasants were shot for harboring Jews (for example, the peasant Zapoz). When the massacre occurred in Breslau (April 3, 1942) we felt that our end was coming.

We escaped with our children over Dryswiaty Lake. A peasant we knew hid us for two months in a garret of a barn.

Because many military personnel passed through there at night, we had to take a rowboat and row for fifteen kilometers. We rowed; I, my wife and three children who were covered with blankets. Because I knew the area well, I was able to navigate the lake. In the morning, we were on the other side, back in Belarus.

We constantly suffered, hiding in farmers' barns and catching colds. We coughed, and therefore could not be hidden there any longer. We dug a ditch and there we lived for five weeks. After many wanderings, we came upon a farmer named Vlatsky. In return for a few sacks of gold, he allowed me to dig a tunnel under a barn attached to his house and there we lived for nineteen months and five days until the Red Army came.

In our hideout there were mice, frogs, worms. We also dug a small hole for defecation and urination. The whole time we did not wash. Lice crawled on our bread.

Testimony of Nachum Kasimow and Musia Levine
October 2, 1945

DIARY
EXCERPTS

AWAKE

14th June 2001
Tel Aviv, Israel

I'm lying on the couch in the living room. The couch is covered with black material around a rosewood frame. It was once covered with beige leather and filled with the finest goose feathers. It is the only piece of furniture that I have brought with me from my former life in the United States. When things become chaotic, I go back to my couch. In each episode of my life, I have lain on a different couch – different colors and hues. In the past, the couches were mostly elegant and exotic. Now, only the frame of this plain black couch recalls more sumptuous times.

Every couch is endowed with different designs from different periods of my life. But they all served the same purpose: a place to hide when things became rough. It does not matter that a couch be fancy or elegant. All that matters is that I can take cover there, as I did during the Nazi occupation of Poland, in our hiding place that we called the Grub ["the pit" or "the grave," in Yiddish]. I use my couch as we used the Grub then, as protection from the world outside.

To feel safe, I need only lie on the couch, almost completely still, and dazed. I sometimes lie for hours, other times for days, without getting up even to eat or drink; only trying to sleep as I did in the

"Grub." I lie on the couch and try to sleep, because it was one of my survival techniques during the Holocaust.

About a week ago, I got in touch with a photographer who wanted to make some sort of film about my Holocaust years. I really feel that I must do something to preserve the memories of my experiences as a child of the Holocaust. I had always planned to write a book; it has been about ten years since I started writing a diary. I planned to finish it sometime, but the years have passed, along with worries about making a living and supporting myself. This left me with no time or means to write. The photographer has asked me to write my story down for the film.

As I lie now on my couch, memories of the Holocaust flood my mind. I am thinking about where to begin. How do I tell the story of the nightmare that turned into a reality and a reality that was a nightmare? How did it all begin? How did it end? The nightmare finished with the end of the war, but it lives on in my memory. It comes in dreams, in all the senses, even smells; it lingers on and on, seeping into every aspect of my life. It is a living entity that follows me, a dark cloud that can catch me at any time, the hunger and fear that deaden the soul, the inhuman conditions of total despair, which came over me one night when I was about eight years old and tried to commit suicide.

The Holocaust experience was so traumatic for a young child in her formative years: the joy of childhood turned into sorrow, woe, fear and hunger – continuous hunger. My childhood innocence was shattered by the horror of the events that I witnessed, by the continuous fear of annihilation by the Nazis – the specter of death that pervaded every moment of my existence.

From left to right: Rita's grandmother's son, Velvl; Rita's grandmother, Mina; Rita's great-grandmother; Rita's grandmother's daughter, Dina, c. 1926

CHILDHOOD IN TURMONT

As I sit to make notes for the documentary film that may or may not be made, memories of my childhood in Turmont, Poland, flood my mind.

I was born into a traditional Jewish family; our original home in Dryswiaty was burned down by the Germans when they occupied Poland in 1941. Our father was building a new home in Dryswiaty, although we also lived in Turmont, in which Father's business was located. We had a big house and my father employed most of the local fishermen; they caught fish and sold all of their catch to him. My father then stored the fish and sold them in various places around Poland, such as Warsaw, Vilna and elsewhere. The house in Turmont was so big that during the Nazi occupation, they turned it into their headquarters and after the war part of it was turned into a pharmacy.

Rita's mother Musia Levine (right) with friend, c. 1930

16th June 2001

June 16th is my date of birth on my passport, July 16th is my birthday on my citizenship papers, and my parents told me that I was born on May 15th. After the war, my father registered us in the town of Turmont. He must have tried to translate the dates from the Jewish into the Roman calendar, and I guess it was confusing for him, after the war, to remember dates and times.

I have few memories from before the war. I was very young. My grandmother lived with us and she was very religious. The house had been made spic and span and the floor had been covered with straw to keep it clean and protected for the Passover Seder. I remember rolling on the floor, and even now, at this moment, I can smell the scent of the fresh straw; or perhaps I am imagining it. At the same time, I also can't help but smell the horrible stench of the Grub, the reeking straw that covered the hole that was our toilet, the stench of urine under me as I lay on the straw in the tunnel that led to the potato bin. I have encountered that smell in the past when I have been in some kind of extreme stress, but it has waned and lost potency with the years.

Another memory from before the war was apparently a traumatic experience for me: I was playing hopscotch. I don't know how it happened, but after I threw the stone and hopped to retrieve it, I jumped on a piece of glass. I went running to my mother who yelled at me; apparently, she blamed me. And at that time her reaction seemed unfair to me.

I was the eldest child, born after a baby boy who died. My parents were very pleased with me. I was the only blonde in the family: fair, cute and precocious. I was apparently very funny, entertaining the whole shtetl by imitating the people of the town. My parents called me Reisale They would say to me, "Reisale, how does Moshe walk?" In response, I'd immediately start limping, and everyone would fall into stitches of laughter and more imitations would follow.

I was born with a lot of energy; I would jump all over the bed, especially my parents' big, brass bed. My father would take out his belt and show me the buckle as a threat. But I did not mind him. I continued to jump. They were concerned that I would break my neck. I was very wild, born wild at heart.

I really rebelled at approximately the age of four and refused to eat anything; you can imagine what this did to a Jewish mother. She fed me cookies for awhile, but I stopped eating even those. As a result, I became malnourished and fell sick with a scalp disease. When the doctors could not cure me, my parents could not cope with me anymore and sent me away to Visigina to stay with my grandparents on their farm (my father's parents were farmers). My grandmother prepared a dish of brown groats for me, baked in milk in the farmer's oven for hours and hours. I liked this and ate it three times a day. I recovered quickly.

My uncle Avraham, the youngest of twelve siblings, helped my grandparents take care of me, to deal with the impetuous *vilde chaye*, as they used to call me. The Holocaust, with all of its horror and tragedy, clipped my wings; it drained some of my wildness away, but not all of it. Later in life, fate and events brought me to situations where my wings were to be clipped again and again.

When I left my grandparents and returned home, the Germans were already occupying Poland.

THE COMING OF THE NAZIS

17th June 2001

In 1942, my parents, my sister Miriam, my brother Harold, and I were placed with five other Jewish families in the ghetto in Dryswiaty, which comprised a few buildings on the outskirts of the town. It was a poor place: women huddled together forced to knit socks for the German soldiers and men toiling hard, digging canals or working on the roads.

One of the first experiences I recall from the beginning of the war was my father returning from a day of forced labor, bleeding heavily from his ear. I remember how shocked we all were. He told us that one of the Nazi overseers had yelled at him and he had not heard. The overseer, furious at being ignored, struck my father with the butt of his rifle. My father never heard well with this ear again. As it was, my father had selective hearing. He did not hear what he did not want to hear. My mother had her ways of testing him, by whispering a mild insult into his ear and waiting to see if he would react.

One day, a priest came and spoke with my father. He told him that all Polish Jews were being rounded up and sent to Ghetto Breslau, where most would be killed. In our region, the Nazis were already lining up Jews in the street and shooting them, so that bodies fell into the canals they had been forced to build. My father related what he had heard to others in the ghetto, but most did not want to listen or believe what he was telling them. My father managed to convince one other family and together, they resolved on a plan to escape and go into hiding. The first thing my father did was arrange for me to go and live with a poor Polish family that lived nearby. They needed money badly, so they readily took the money that my father paid them. And since I was blond and could speak Polish, they were willing to take the chance and allow me to stay with them. My father now had fewer people to conceal when the time came to escape. My younger sister had dark features and was easily recognizable as Jewish, and my brother was too young to be sent away; he was only a baby.

I don't remember a word of Polish now; it was all erased after a traumatic experience in the ghetto.

18*th* June 2001

I am sitting in a coffeehouse next to the sea; it is called Frishman, which is also the name of the street on which I live. The cafe is only half a block from my home and my home is only half a block from the sea. I am looking at the waves as they break along the shore. The beach is noisy and full of bathers: men, women and children. I am able to block out the noise and concentrate solely on the waves. I love coffeehouses; I find the aroma of the coffee, combined with the waves breaking gently on the shore, brings me to a kind of meditative state.

A memory comes to my mind: an image from another time, in another world, almost, from a different planet. I remember a frozen lake covered with snow. It is nighttime. I am riding with my father in a sleigh, which is being pulled by two horses, as if in a fairy tale. I can hear the horses' bells jingling happily. It is dark, but the moon casts its shimmer on to the frozen, snow-covered surface of the lake. I can see the sprinkled lights of the fishermen as they sit scattered across the lake, fishing through holes in the ice, their lanterns twinkling in the night.

Now, tears come to my eyes and begin to fall down my cheeks and onto the pages on which I write. I have to reach for my sunglasses and put them on so that people don't see me cry. These recollections of moments in a lost time have become encapsulated in my mind. I will never forget those wonderful times before the Germans occupied Poland, before they destroyed the beauty of my world and took away the innocence of my childhood. I continue to cry and feel the acute pain that is so very hard to describe. I am grieving for a world lost forever: the stillness of that night, the stars, the full moon shining above, the jingle of the bells, the white snow beneath the gliding sleigh with my father sitting beside me, the lanterns glittering across the lake, reflecting light and shining on the white snow.

I wish I were a poet and could express the ineffable pleasure of that moment, the way I felt it as a child. The moments of bliss are stored in memory, along with so many other painful recollections. Traumatic events may, at times, dominate our memories and feelings more than positive experiences.

These feelings drain my energy, making me drowsy and I

cannot keep my eyes open. I am sitting across the street in my neighborhood coffeehouse. I am drinking a caffe latte and eating a delicious cheesecake. I am trying to keep myself awake so that I can write in my diary. I call this my "morning papers." I cannot always write in the mornings; it is four o'clock in the afternoon now. I am mostly not really awake these days. Lately, I don't really want to work or teach anymore. What I really want to do is paint and write and sit in coffeehouses or meet with friends. Coffeehouses wake me up a bit. I must wake up and do things. "Rita, wake up, life is short!"

Ever since the recent Intifada began, I have felt that time may run out on me. I have so much to give and if I don't publish something or make a film, all these experiences will be erased. They need to be remembered.

I cannot go through life half-asleep. However, sleeping is one of the survival techniques I used during the Holocaust and still use to this day. When I slept as a child in the Grub, I could dream of the wonderful little cakes that my mother used to bake, of halva and Jaffa oranges that my father used to bring back from his business trips in Vilna. The smell was very exotic, wrapped in an interesting orange wrapper. I always dreamed of eating delicious food, "wish fulfillment," as Freud called it. The longer I slept then, the longer I could forget about the nightmare reality. Why wake up?

The aroma of coffee fills my nose and fresh-baked cakes fill the shelves. I am in the land of milk and honey. I can eat as many oranges, cakes, and slices of halva as I like, every day if I wish, whenever my heart desires. The hunger of a Holocaust child's dreams are fulfilled, but it does not satisfy another hunger, a hunger that cannot be satisfied by food.

What are my hungers, my desires, and my goals now? Has my life been a series of survival techniques, and not actual living? So what is living? Some have said that I had it all or still have it all: children, grandchildren, husbands, lovers, houses and cars. I even had money at some time in the past. Inside, though, I feel like I've lived in a castle with no foundation.

My grandchildren get up and brush their teeth, go to school, come home to a beautiful house, and then go off to activities. My memories as a child are images of horror, death, hunger, fear, and more fear… I can't remember years or dates; they are all jumbled together. There was no frame of reference for me, like my children and grandchildren have. You get up at a certain hour, go to sleep at a certain hour, and fill up your days with activities: school, computer games, television, videos and of course birthday parties, swimming trips, and the best food that money can buy. No structure such as this was built into my formative years. Sleep was the nearest I came to pleasure. I woke into darkness and hunger, and went to sleep in darkness and hunger.

The Holocaust is over; it is really over. But is it for me? Why do I continue to need to sleep and sleep when life is stressful? Awake Rita, Awake! The Holocaust is over!

19th June 2001

I was sleeping on the black couch in the living room, the radio switched on with news of the Intifada. I feel very lethargic. I really do not want to wake up to another day of Intifada. It is not fear that keeps me asleep like in the Holocaust, but a disturbing feeling that things are changing, and not for the better. I am not afraid for my personal safety. I am afraid for my children and grandchildren, for my people, and for the land of Israel. The reasons for my not having any fear for my own personal safety are another story.

It's good to get out of the stifling heat of my apartment. The air-conditioning has broken down, and it will cost too much money to get it fixed. I wish that I had enough money so that I would not have to worry about such things. A weakness descends over me when I start to think about the realities of everyday life – I want to go to sleep and hide from everything.

A memory comes to me from another hiding place in my childhood in the midst of the Holocaust. As I mentioned earlier, my father took me from the ghetto in Dryswiaty to stay with a

Christian family that was very poor, the poorest of all the farmers in the area. I remember their house, which was more like a hut. It had a domed tin roof with tin walls and a cold, hard earth floor. Inside, there was a big oven and an alcove above it, where I would hide from the two sons of the family. They used to chase me and beat me up when their mother was not around. The mother liked me, because I was very obedient and learned quickly. She taught me to say the Lord's Prayer until I knew it by heart; she had tried to teach it to her sons for years – they were both older than me – but had had no success with them. She used to call them all kinds of names, none of which I can recall now, and used to scold them for not being as quick or obedient as I was. Sometimes the boys caught me before I could hide on top of the alcove of the oven and they would beat me. I was so afraid of them, but I never told their mother that they abused me. I can't remember my feelings exactly, but I can vividly imagine them now.

I was then as I am now, very imaginative.

I remember Christmas time in that small hut. The mother told me stories about Jesus Christ and I remember that I liked those stories. On Christmas Eve, after we had eaten the Christmas dinner, I remember we had some red jelly that was supposed to be symbolic in some way. After we had eaten, I went up to the small ledge above the oven to wait for the baby Jesus to be born; for some reason, I expected that he would be born right there on the table in the house. I woke up in the middle of the night and saw in my imagination, although I thought it was real at the time, an image of the baby Jesus in a basket on the table. I remember being awake and curious, but did not go down from my ledge to have a closer look.

A few weeks later, a man came into the house (or rather, hut; you cannot call it a house). He looked at me and said, "Isn't that Nochim's little girl?" A lot of the Christian people knew my father, since many of them worked for him as fishermen. I think that the polish woman mumbled some story that I was a cousin or something like that. The next day, my father came and took me back to the small Jewish ghetto in Dryswiaty.

The next morning, I woke up and saw my grandmother praying. She would stand praying all day, mostly from a book of *Tehillim* (Psalms). That is how I remember her, standing and praying. I remember that I wanted to pray with her, and as the woman in the tin hut had taught me, I made the sign of the holy cross and dropped to my knees and began to pray. I noticed my grandmother looking at me in a way that frightened me. I do not remember what happened next. I was told that she fainted and from then on I decided never to speak Polish again and consequently the Polish language was erased from my mind.

I remember promising myself that I would learn all of the Jewish prayers. I fulfilled my promise to study Judaism by graduating from the Jewish Theological Seminary of New York with a bachelor's degree in religious studies. I also taught Judaism and Hebrew in Jewish schools in the United States.

I cannot recall a word of Polish now, although I understood and spoke it as a child. An inertia or lack of motivation has come over me. I have to force myself to get up. I feel so alone in all of these memories and feelings that engulf my mind.

Wake up, Rita! Wake up! Just do it! The universe likes action, not laziness. The show must go on no matter what. But why, at this moment, is it so hard for me to remember? Why?

I get up and make myself a cup of coffee.

20th June 2001

I must continue writing and painting this time. I must continue and not stop like I have in the past. Time seems to be running out on me. I start, I continue and commit myself along the way and then I stop. I delay for a month or maybe a year and then start again from the beginning, with a lot of guilt and regret that I did not continue in the first place. I have perpetuated this cycle all my life; I must change and stop this destructive procrastination.

What I want is to put into words the material inside me; and my hope is that it will emerge from the dark clouds. I have so much to offer and all of it has remained hidden – like me. I must come out of hiding and show myself to the world. I must open myself up to new experiences and stop living in this coma. The war is over; I can wake up and come out of hiding.

The Intifada is gaining momentum. There have been many times when I've been afraid to leave my television; I worry that if I switch it off, another terrible thing will happen. It is as though I believe that by watching the television continuously, it will stop bad things from happening! Coincidentally, this has happened a few times. I don't listen for a few hours, and then I switch on the television or turn on the radio, and horrible things have happened – a *piguah* (terrorist attack). Innocent people, babies, the young, and the old, wounded or killed by suicide bombers. When will this bloodshed end?

I am not afraid of suicide bombers. There is some kind of omnipotent feeling accompanying this statement. I feel that I am invincible; if Hitler did not get me, then a suicide bomber or terrorist won't succeed where he failed. Of course, I will die – eventually we all do – but I know now that I will not die young.

My father used to say that to me when I worried about him running around and working like a young man at the age of eighty-five. He was a real hero. He died at the age of ninety with a new girlfriend by his side. My mother had died fifteen years earlier, at the age of seventy-five.

I have so much to say about my father, but if I do this now, I will start to cry. I want to keep my hopes up. I want to make a film and write a book. I know that it will give me solace when my stories see the light and I know that my memories will never be erased.

22nd June 2001

I woke up early in the morning in Salit, in the home of my son's family. The first thing I noticed was an incredible new painting in the dining room, which I hadn't noticed when I came in late the previous night. The painting depicts sheep in many different colors. I was amazed by the composition of the colors and found that I could not stop gazing at it. Incredibly, two of my paintings were on either side of this wonderful painting by Kadishman. My daughter-in-law loves my paintings, but it is hard to believe that these paintings, hanging beside a real Kadishman, are mine.

The previous days I have spent with my grandchildren: playing, talking, cooking, painting pictures for them, and laughing all the while. All three of them have so much humor. I love them and they love me: it is such a privilege to be with them and it is delightful to be hugged by them.

I sit down to write at the dining room table, opposite the Kadishman. No one is at home right now; my grandchildren are visiting friends. They are all very sociable. The youngest insists on inviting friends or else going to them himself. He is very determined to get what he wants; he is not interested in excuses such as "your friend is not home" or "not today." These realities are not relevant to him. He gets what he wants and that is it.

I find it difficult to believe in my accomplishments. I look out of the bay window into a beautiful garden full of blooming flowers, green bushes, and lightly swaying trees. It is very quiet, as everyone is still asleep. I walk out into the garden. The air is fresh and the view is clear. I can see the Arab villages in the surrounding area. Soon, the muezzin will call Muslims to prayer. I take a deep breath of the fresh air and sit down with a cup of coffee. How wonderful to be sitting here, in this Garden of Eden, breathing the fresh air.

My grandchildren went to school looking beautiful, nicely dressed, with smiling faces; everything is picturesque outside, and quiet and lovely inside. So why am I crying? My tears are running down onto the page that I'm writing and my weeping, bursting out from deep inside me, is so loud that I scare away the two cats that were sleeping peacefully on the couch. I had no childhood. I had no clothes, I had no food, no school, only hunger and fear, hunger and fear. The Nazis murdered my childhood. And now the memory comes back to me.

The priest informed my father that we were to be transported in a day or so to the Widze ghetto, and from there to Breslau, a larger ghetto, and that a lot of us would be killed (at that time even the priest did not know about the concentration camps). That night, we escaped from the small ghetto in Dryswiaty – my father and my mother with three young children.

My parents never wanted to talk to us about what happened to our grandmother and to all our other family members who were annihilated, but they always talked in Yiddish between themselves. Years later, when my family had relocated to New York, I decided I had to talk about our beautiful grandmother and I asked my father what happened to her after we escaped. My father told me that once we knew we had to flee, my grandmother insisted that we run away without her. She said that she would go together with the others to Widze, where she would see her son Velvl and her daughter Dina with their families, who lived nearby. Having no choice, my father fled with his three small children. My grandmother met her end at the hands of the Nazi murderers with all the other members of the family. (Her picture can be found on page 5.)

My family and I were in the woods and perhaps twenty or more other people, who were hiding with us in the caves. I was choking from the smell of so many people pressed together in one small cave. Some children cried, and their parents almost had to choke them to keep them quiet. Some of the things I saw and heard in that cave are not for a child's eyes and ears, and surely not for the young and impressionable young girl that I was. I cannot even write them in my diary, and perhaps I never will. The pictures and images in my memory have not been erased; they reappear at unexpected moments.

As I'm writing this, I'm trying desperately not to cry. Tears are running down my cheeks and onto the table. I look up and I see the rays of sunshine blurred through my tears; light floods through the flowers and bushes, reflecting the brilliant colors of the garden. The stillness of the moment embraces me, while my chest heaves with pain, tears flowing even harder. I control my sobs so as not to wake my family. The only noise I can hear, aside from the beating of my heart, is a bee buzzing annoyingly. I put my head on the table and cry bitterly, my chest heaving rhythmically. I stop writing.

CORRESPONDENCE WITH "JAY"

27th June 2001

"Jay" came to me in a dream in 1984, when my life was in chaos. Jay is a figure I sometimes dialogue with, using Carl Jung's notion of "active imagination." This letter below is an example of active imagination.

> Dear Jay,
>
> I haven't written to you for months, and for that, I am sorry. I hope everything is well with you and your family. Many months have passed without my writing in my diary, since meeting with the photographer who is interested in making a film about my Holocaust experiences, I have become motivated to write again and reconnect all the events in my memory.
>
> I have an urgent need to express all the memories, events, and after-effects of my Holocaust experience. I don't feel like hiding anymore. I want these feelings to come to light. In the end, I found out that we could not find common ground to go ahead with this project. It was shelved to continue some other time in the future. However, I'm painting and writing again and hoping to make exhibitions of my paintings. I also wrote a play called *From the Hell and Death of the Holocaust to the Land of the Free*.
>
> Yours truly,
> Rita

23rd July 2001

Dear Jay,

I wrote to you on June 27th and I haven't heard from you yet. I hope you and your family are OK, and I look forward to hearing from you.

I assume you must be very famous by now throughout Paris. I wish you could come and visit me in Israel. When you go outside at this time of year, it's like being in a sauna. My clothes become wet from perspiring so much. My air-conditioning has broken down and it costs too much money to fix.

The Intifada is also heating up more and more everyday; there seems to be no end. The terrorists are planning more and more suicide attacks all over Israel, especially in the big cities like Tel Aviv and Jerusalem; inside the Green Line, outside the Green Line, there are no limits to their killing. In Tel Aviv, the restaurants and coffeehouses are still full with people laughing and enjoying themselves; the show must go on. We cannot let the terrorists disrupt our lives. They want us to leave this country, our homeland.

I haven't written in my diary for a month. I have all kinds of excuses – good excuses, but excuses all the same. I must go back to writing in my diary, at least a few pages three or four times each week. I have to promise myself this, and stick to it.

You know how easily I become discouraged and abandon projects that I have invested a lot of time and energy in and that means that I am stopping myself from enjoying the fruits of my labor. Why do I destroy my chances of real success? There are theories about the psychological processes connected to success and failure, but I am not sure that any of them could be attributed to me; I don't know.

On Tuesday, I am meeting with the photographer

for another interview for the film. I'm giving him another chance regarding the film, this isn't easy for me, not so much in telling the story but in his not listening to it.

I told him about the Grub, which was our last hiding place before the liberation by the Russians. We lived in the Grub for nineteen months and five days in hunger and darkness, engulfed by the horrendous smells, the continuous fears, overshadowed by more traumatic events and increasing fear of the Nazis.

Write soon.

Regards to your family.

Love,

Rita

30th July 2001

Dear Rita,

It was good to hear from you again, as I had not heard anything from you for the past few years.

I am so glad that you decided to wake up and stop sleepwalking through your life. It is not that I judge you. Believe me, I know what you went through in the Grub and that through sleep, you saved your life and your sanity. This survival technique is one of the defenses that one falls back on when things are bad in one's life or when one feels threatened in some way.

You continuously berate yourself for not doing enough. Of course you can do more, everyone can. You are doing many creative things, such as painting and writing. Even your teaching is creative, "Creative Processes through the Arts" being the title of the subject you are teaching at the University of Haifa. How much more creative can you be? You are working with patients, teaching at the university, and you are writing a play that may be only the first part of a trilogy.

You mentioned that you are currently involved in the production of a film based on your Holocaust experience. Some of these things are new challenges for you. Trying new things takes a lot of courage, too – and you complain about your writing ability! To think that you are even contemplating writing two more plays – wow!

Yes, there are risks, but don't forget the many times you have jumped into things headlong and have succeeded. Of course, sometimes one fails, you cannot prevent failure. These are the things that you want to do in your life and right now, you are doing them – I think this will help you in your soul-searching. It is amazing how you do not lose faith and continue to attempt these creative things. I wish you the best of luck and hope that you continue to flourish and do not, as has been the case in the past, become surrounded by people who discourage you and interfere in the relationships you have with the people and things that you love.

Many times you have asked me why these things happen to you. There are many theories: God's will, karma, and erroneous choices. We should figure this out together one day. It may be that we won't ever establish the cause, but what is more important is to find a way to prevent these things from recurring and irreparably damaging your life.

My advice to you is to remember to give yourself the occasional pat on the back and remind yourself often that you are OK! You are not lazy: for a so-called lazy person, you do an awful lot! Try to eradicate these feelings of inadequacy and non-achievement – they serve no purpose other than hindering you on your journey.

Well, I am getting along well, I am getting grayer with worrying about my sick, aging parents, the clinic, the children, etc. You can, however, congratulate me on the birth of my granddaughter. My daughter married a nice Jewish boy – Thank God!

Yours,

Jay

THE "GRUB"

31st July 2001

I am sitting in my kitchen and looking out of the window, a large window that looks out onto Beit-El synagogue. Between my window and the synagogue grows a huge ancient tree with many swaying branches. In bloom, the tree is spectacular! There are some branches that touch my window; it seems that each branch offers me a handful of pretty red blossoms. The prayers from the synagogue drift up through my window and fill my home with their melodic notes, sent forth by the cantor and his congregation.

I feel that I must continue recording my memories and reflections of the Holocaust; the producer will need more details when we next meet and I want to be ready. At this moment, I feel that my pen is writing of its own free will; it is an extension my mind, working independently of my hand, as it flows forward filling the pages. My mind is overloaded with memories; I don't even have to think. I am hoping that it will clear some space in my mind. But, as I know from experience, the memories will return of their own will.

After we left the caves, we joined with another family, and together, we hid in a cattle feed barn for four or five months. The family with whom we hid was neither fair nor nice; they kept the larger portions of the little food we had.

When my father realized this, he went looking for another hiding place. He was gone for a few days, perhaps a week – I don't recall exactly. When he returned, we learned that he had visited another Polish family with whom he was acquainted, a Christian family that owned a farm in a rural area called Malaki. They seemed sympathetic to our plight and allowed my father to dig a hiding place for us in their cattle shed. The farmer's family was very poor and needed the gold my father gave them to hide us.

My father dug a cave in the ground in the stable. It was a little longer than his own height, and not very deep: my baby brother Harold was the only one able to stand up inside. Inside the Grub, there was only enough space to lie down flat: my father, mother, brother and sister lying side by side while I lay in a tunnel that led to the potato bin. At one end of the Grub, as I mentioned, there was a small hole dug into the ground that served as our toilet, which my father would cover with a ball of straw in an attempt to block out its stench. I hated the toilet in the Grub. When the straw cover was removed, bullfrogs covered with feces would jump out: they terrified and disgusted me. I would not use that hole unless it was absolutely necessary: instead, I would urinate on the straw beneath me as I lay.

My father understood my fear and changed my straw as regularly as he could. At the other end was a narrow tunnel that led to the place where potatoes were stored in an underground bin; this was opened by a trapdoor that led into the framer's bedroom. It was in this tunnel that I used to lie. The earth beneath me was covered with straw. The ceiling looked like a cave, with only a sliver of light in the corner from the barn above. This was the only source of light we had.

We also called the Grub *"Kever,"* which is Yiddish for grave. It was well-named, for that is what it was: a grave in which we endured our living death – hunger, fear and more hunger for almost two years. When I think of the Grub now, I do not know how we survived in that horrible place; it was a nightmare, obliterating the essence of being human.

I remember being in New York with a friend, also a Holocaust survivor and when we first came across *The Diary of Anne Frank*, I recall saying that Frank's hiding place was a Hilton compared to our Grub. Anne Frank would certainly have become a great writer if the Nazis had not killed her. The Holocaust deprived the world of so much talent and potential. I am thankful that I survived and am alive and writing my diary today.

1st August 2001

Dear Jay,

I called the photographer today to arrange a meeting so that we could finish our business. I had thought that by this time we would already have begun making the film. Working with him was so frustrating; I invested my time and energy into the project, but saw clearly that nothing would be accomplished. So this time, I listened to your advice and ended our association in time, before it became frustrating. He wanted compensation for the hours that he had put in and I paid him. I agreed to all of his requests so that we could finish in an amicable way.

I could feel him clipping my wings. At times, when I had an optimistic or creative thought about the film he would dampen it by telling me that I should not talk like that. You know how much I hate it when people try to shut me up when I am being creative. I feel that they are trying to take away a precious gift that God gave me – communication.

I am suddenly saddened by this thought: it is disheartening to think that I will now have to look for someone else to do the film. I feel so alone in all of this; I have no support from anyone.

Yours,
Rita

3rd August 2001

It is Friday morning and I am sitting in my kitchen. The apartment is flooded with light from all the windows. In the kitchen, there is a huge window that stretches from one wall to the other. Looking out I behold the old synagogue and the ancient tree that has grown toward my window and above to meet me. The synagogue, the tree, and my apartment are on Frishman Street in Tel Aviv. This morning, I opened all the windows and took down all the curtains and blinds so I could see outside. The air is so fresh.

A memory comes to mind from the Grub. I remember the horrible stench of the place, the darkness, but most of all the gnawing hunger that seemed to have no end and all too quickly turned to pain. I can almost feel that desperate hunger at this moment; I take a sip of my coffee. I love coffee. I have already eaten breakfast this morning. I remember lying on the stinking, wet straw drenched in urine; the stinking toilet, the bullfrogs, the terrible odor that followed me into later life whenever I was under stress.

In 1977, when I was training at a private clinic in Israel to become a psychotherapist, I told the psychiatrist with whom I was working about the recurring memory of that smell, while I was assisting him in a group therapy session. He told me not to mention it to the group, as it would upset them.

Later, I went to another private clinic for help and they told me that I should think of it as an inflamed appendix that could not be healed and would, from time to time, flare up. There was nothing that could be done about it, so therefore I should accept it.

Of course, at that time they did not know how to treat Holocaust survivors. Nowadays there are miles and miles of shelves filled with books and articles on the subject. But I doubt that there really can be a cure for such horrific experiences of real-life nightmare in a surrealistic world.

In 1991, I worked as an art therapist with psychotic patients and Holocaust survivors in a closed psychiatric ward in an Israeli hospital. The survivors saw Nazis hanging from the ceiling, sitting at the window and hiding in every corner. There was nowhere else for them to go; they were alone, without any kind of financial support. We did all we could to try to help these people, but what could we really do? We all felt that the Holocaust survivors did not belong in the hospital, but rather, in a private sanatorium. No such place existed then and the patients were too sick to fight for their rights.

The people with whom I worked were devoted professionals. The head of the department was an enlightened and knowledgeable man; I feel privileged to have worked with him. He really believed in me and there was joy and openness in our relationship. The sessions he supervised were a real eye-opener for me. I felt encouraged, appreciated and enriched under his supervision. He had so many talents: creativity, intelligence and profound understanding.

7th August 2001

I am on a train traveling from Tel Aviv to Haifa. Trees, green bushes and buildings flash by as I stare out the window. Haifa station is approaching, and I already see the familiar sights of the beach and the sea. I turn to look out the other side and see clusters of houses built on the slopes of Mount Carmel. On the horizon, like an ancient obelisk standing high on the hill, I see the University of Haifa. Some people call it "The White Elephant," as well as other unflattering names; it does not fit in at all with its surroundings.

Up there, on the twentieth floor, is my office. I teach once a week, for five hours, a course I created myself: "Creative Processes through the Arts." I will not explain what it is, because I am not sure that I can. It is art, drama, psychology, philosophy; it is East meets West, and more. I love teaching it, because so far I have been given the freedom to do whatever I want. My students are intelligent and beautiful. The head of the department is very impressed with some of the techniques I use. Once, when I discussed with him some of the goals I had set myself and the techniques I planned to use, he laughed at me and told me that they would never work with Israeli male students. Nevertheless I did teach my lessons as I had planned and succeeded. My students loved the course and I loved them all very much; they gave me hope for the future, for a better world.

It's getting increasingly harder for me to make the trip every week from Tel Aviv to Haifa, then a long drive to my friend's house, where I prepare for the lesson, stay overnight, teach my class, drag myself (along with a great many art materials) back to Tel Aviv. I get home around nine o'clock in the evening if I am lucky.

Today I am going to Haifa to do some private work. My friends tell me that at my age, people sit on benches, complaining about operations they underwent and treatments they are receiving. I, on the other hand, am involved in writing a book or two, dating, teaching, and babysitting my grandchildren. I have to be grateful to God, and I am grateful, but what about my childhood? Where was He then, when I cried to Him for help? "God save me and my family and all the Jewish people from this hell," I prayed. I cannot and could not imagine anywhere that could be worse than the Grub.

I sat outside the tunnel with my feet still inside; I did not want to be anywhere near the so-called toilet. I sat rocking back and forth, as if in prayer. My sister, brother and I were shaved, so as not to get lice. I was dressed in a coarse linen nightgown. My days were spent waking up from sleep into hunger, and trying to go back to sleep. Eventually, some food would be sent down to the Grub via the potato bin. Usually, it was some kind of mixture of beans that the farmer cooked to feed his rabbits. The farmer threw us the rabbit's leftovers.

10*th* August 2001
A telephone call from Jay.

JAY: Hi, Rita. Thank you for your letters. I am always pleasantly surprised to hear from you, but am sad to hear that you are very lonely these days. Bear in mind that you can turn to me whenever you feel like it. Count on me for support in healing you, as I have done in the past. Do you remember the Pasteur Clinic in Paris, where you came to consult me on your way to San Francisco? You were at a crossroads then and I healed your knee so that you could walk again. And I'm pleased in thinking that I was able to help you.

RITA: Of course I remember, Jay. But you are just a dream figure. What can you do for me now? I feel so lost and alone in everything.

JAY: There is some creative process going on when you dialogue with me; perhaps it is catharsis or an authentic dialogue with yourself.

RITA: Dialoguing with you may help a little, or as you put it, "dialoguing with the inner healer," but I need more concrete help. I need financial support; my overdraft in the bank is growing, and I don't know what to do. It scares me more than the Intifada. I survived Hitler and the Grub; I will survive the terrorists. I am worried about my children, my grandchildren, my people, and my country.

JAY: I wonder why you don't seem to write much about the Intifada?

RITA: I am living with it, as you know. There are many nights when I am glued to the television and then my world only gets darker. It is so painful to see the bloodshed. I really don't want to talk about it; I only become more nervous and upset, so please don't ask me. I'm sure you know what is going on here.

JAY: Still, you have a lot to be thankful for, Rita: you have your health, your work, and all of the creative things that you are working on. I am pleased to hear that you have almost finished your first play; I know that you have never done a project like this before. I remember that you were always complaining that you could not write – and you say that you plan to write two more plays! Perhaps you will go on with this documentary film when you are through with the photographer you do not like. I think you are right in saying that he was wrong for you; as you say, he tried to clip your wings, and this would have been destructive. This time, however, you stopped it in time.

RITA: Yes, I did. Thank you very much for the good advice that you gave me.

JAY: There is no need to thank me; thank yourself for the good things that you are doing to help yourself.

RITA: Give my love to your family and thank you for calling. I am grateful for all of the advice you give me, although sometimes I think that I should follow it more closely.

JAY: Be well. Take better care of yourself than you have done lately. I will call you again soon to see how you are doing. I will be watching the news and if things get quieter over there, I may come for a lecture; if so, I will visit you.

RITA: Don't build your hopes up that things will settle down soon; I fear that maybe the situation will become worse before it gets better. But please visit me. In Tel Aviv, people are still doing all the things that they did before the Intifada: the restaurants and coffeehouses are filled with young and old, the beaches are packed with bathers. We all must go on with our lives; otherwise we will become weak and our enemies may destroy us. We pay dearly every day with bloodshed, sorrow and mourning; yet my feeling is that we can survive it all. Oh well, I don't really want to talk about it, so goodnight, Jay, and thanks for calling.

JAY: Goodnight, Rita. Sleep well, and have pleasant dreams. We will continue to talk in the future.

18th August 2001
A Dream

This morning, I woke from a horrible dream – a Nazi dream. It has been years since I last had a Nazi dream. It was a short dream and I can only recall a few images from it. I dream that I am sitting with two groups of people: one German, one Polish. I recognize a face from the German group; he is one of my neighbors: a young German tourist, who lives across the hall from me. He always smiles and says *Shalom* and asks me how I am. In my dream, however, he is part of the German group. I can feel that both groups are hostile toward me; I feel frightened by them. Both groups speak to me, saying, "You will all be dead in six months." I wake up shattered.

Associations of the Dream

I often reflect on my dreams and try to understand their meaning. Perhaps this dream means that I am afraid of the Intifada. It has been quite a while since I experienced this kind of fear. But then, I say to myself that it was only a dream and death can also mean rejuvenation and change: perhaps, the end of a certain episode in my life and the beginning of a new one.

I pray that God will grant me the time to continue with my creative work and give me the strength to overcome all the obstacles occurring on the way. Maybe my dream is my unconscious telling me that time is short, that I must hurry to complete my projects.

After the war, I used to have many Nazi dreams, dreams that they were chasing me, wanting to annihilate me, to murder me. I think it is strange that in the Grub I did not suffer from these nightmares; I dreamt of the things that I longed for, such as food, nice clothes, and tea parties with my friends. Freud called this "dream fulfillment."

The unconscious works in strange and mysterious ways that we cannot yet understand. The reality of living in the Grub was such a nightmare that maybe my unconscious saved me from the terror of Nazi nightmares, while coping with so much trauma and imminent threat. My unconscious let me dream of all the pleasures I longed for and it was only after we left the Grub that the Nazi nightmares began.

I used to have the nightmares nearly every night; I would wake up screaming and sometimes find that I had been sleepwalking. I had to be comforted and calmed before I could fall asleep again. In my nightmares, the Nazi terror was re-enacted with a frightening sense of reality. My life was free from suffering and fear, but the Nazis continued to wreak havoc and terrorize me by night; I now know that this was post-traumatic stress.

I remember one night, after we had left our home in Turmont and were traveling by train to the displaced persons (DP) camps in Germany. I was sleeping on the floor of the train and I woke up screaming so loudly from a nightmare, that the people on the top bunks of our compartment fell from their beds in shock. Later, those people complained to my father that I had disturbed their sleep. They said that I was probably crazy and should be taken to see a psychiatrist. I remember having a wonderful laugh with my sister about the two people falling out of their beds and thumping onto the floor.

The symbols that recurred most in my dreams were the images of the Nazi boots and the insignia on the Nazi hats. The Nazi soldier was never a human being to me – neither in real life, nor in my dreams. Rather, they were faceless terrors that were identifiable only by their uniforms. My young mind seemed to have saved me from the disturbing truth that these men were in fact human, as much flesh and blood as I, or even my mother and father, and yet they had caused indescribable pain and untold loss of life. I think that I segregated the Nazis in my unconscious mind as quite different from all humanity, dehumanizing them in order to cope with all the horrors and suffering they caused to the Jewish people during the Holocaust.

After my son was born, the terrifying nightmares stopped. I think my life was altered so profoundly by giving birth to a new life that my unconscious was affected as much as my conscious. I still had many dreams that contained Nazi elements, but these elements manifested themselves more as symbols than images of terror.

I remember a dream that I had in September last year: I am sitting on the side of a highway and wondering how I am going to cross it. The highway is huge; it consists of eight lanes, all full of traffic traveling very fast in the same direction. As I am sitting thinking about how to cross, all of the cars stop so that I can cross. As I begin to make my way across the road, I feel that I am unable to continue walking or even to stand up. I look down and realize that I am wearing tall, masculine, black leather boots, which are very heavy. I begin to crawl and finally manage to cross all eight lanes of the highway. I only have to cross a small exit to reach the other side. I feel that I can do this without any problems.

Association
Luckily, the dream was set in the U.S., so the people in the cars were patient enough to wait for me to crawl across. Also, lucky for me that it was not in Israel, where the drivers would not have had the patience to let me cross slowly! The boots symbolized the Nazi murderers and it was a recurring image in my nightmares. This horror image followed me with intent to kill, until the birth of my son. But I'm still in the above dream. I'm still encumbered with heavy boots that impede my progress in life. In the end I make it across the highway, but on my knees.

19th August 2001
The train is moving from Tel Aviv to Haifa: my weekly trip. I am sitting in a comfortable blue chair in an air-conditioned coach. There are soldiers in uniform all around; they sometimes stick their rifles or Uzis in my ribs, unintentionally of course. Despite what people say about sabras, they are polite as they help me with my bags; they give me a feeling of safety. I look out of the window at the scenery flashing by. I listen to the rhythm of the train and I remember a time when I was on another train journey. The grown-ups had taken all the

beds, so I lay on the floor and listened to the rhythm of the train as it sped along. My ear pressed to the floor, the noise was loud in my ear.

I remember when we first went into the Grub. At first, it was hard to see anything, but as our eyes became accustomed to the dark and light seeped through the straw above us, I could see my family clearly. At first, the farmer gave us sufficient quantities of food, as he thought that the war would be over in a few months. But then, as it dragged on, he realized that he was stuck with us, so he designed a plan to poison us. My mother developed excellent hearing, sitting in the potato bin and listening to what went on in the farmer's house above. She overheard their plan to rid themselves of their burden – us. At least the farmer would not have to worry about burying us, as we were already living in a grave. My mother told my father what she had overheard, and my father, with his insight and determination to survive, developed his counter plan. He went to tell the *goy*, the farmer, that he was going to meet with his brother Avraham, who was hiding in the woods with the partisans, and that he would be away for a few days. Of course, my father did not find my uncle Avraham, but told the farmer that he had, and that he had told the partisans where we were hiding. The farmer was now in a quandary: if he killed us, the partisans would find out and take revenge; if the Germans found us, they would burn his farm and kill him and his family. He must have decided to leave us and take the chance that the Nazis would not find us.

My father used to leave the Grub to go out and search for food. I remember that every time he left, we were terrified: each time Father left, he was in mortal danger, and so were we: what would happen to us if something happened to him and he did not return?

27th August 2001

Dear Jay,

This is the first time that I have written a play, having found it very hard to finish. I find that as I write, all of the memories well up in my mind. I have been betrayed so many times, and even to this day I am suffering from betrayal. It affects me so much that I cannot even write you about it. Both my first and second husbands betrayed me, as did some of my friends. I can feel my strength being sapped just by thinking about it; you can imagine what a devastating effect each one had on me at the time.

I have never betrayed anyone; I have always been straight and honest with people. So why does this have to happen to me? My life seems to have been a string of betrayals. I suffer just mentioning it. I cannot bring myself to go into details; it just hurts too much.

Please write soon.

Yours,

Rita

14th September 2001

Dear Jay,

I haven't written to you or in my diary for two weeks. So much is happening in my life and in Israel at the moment, and now the terrible attacks on the World Trade Center in New York and the Pentagon in Washington. Under these conditions, I do not feel inclined to sit down and write about myself.

I'm sure you must have seen on your television in Paris the horrible pictures from New York and Washington. I myself was glued to the TV from the time it happened until late that night. My eyes stung from crying so much; all my energy drained away and was replaced by a deadening sensation through the whole of my body.

I tried to call my sister in New York, but evidently the lines were overloaded and I couldn't get through. I managed to speak with my brother in Iowa, and he told me that he had spoken with her and assured me that she was OK. I immediately relaxed. I can remember how frightened she was when she lived in Israel and the Yom Kippur War broke out. She immediately left Israel and flew back to the States with her son. I, on the other hand, had no fear for my personal safety during the Yom Kippur War or the Gulf War or even of the Intifada, for that matter. I fear only for my family, my country, and my people.

During the Yom Kippur War, I sent my children down to the basement and asked my neighbors to take care of them. I stayed on the eleventh floor of our apartment building in Israelia, Haifa. I told my children and my neighbors that I would not go down to any cellar or bunker to hide from bombs. There was no one in the whole building; I was alone in the apartment, listening to the radio, while airplanes and helicopters flew overhead. I heard a helicopter fly directly over our building and my heart began to beat faster, because I knew that it was carrying the wounded soldiers to the nearby Rambam Hospital.

I was in a synagogue with my children when the announcement came that war had broken out. We walked slowly back to our building, where I sent the children to the shelter as we had been instructed to do. As for myself I knew that I could not go with them; come what may, nothing would force me to hide in bunkers, cellars or shelters, ever again.

During the Gulf War, I put on a gas mask for about half an hour, but then I took it off, as it would be useless against bombs. The next day, as soon as we were allowed to go outside, I went out to comfort my friends who were very frightened. They are not Holocaust survivors.

I don't know whether it is a false illusion of invulnerability, but I do know that my reaction to fear stems from my experience during the Holocaust. During moments of intensity, my fear seems to quickly burn itself out and leave behind a hollow space. I may not make myself clear as I find it very difficult to explain.

When surrounded by fear, I say to myself, "No more, no more. I have had enough. What is the worst that could happen? I could die, but so what? We all die sometime."

I recall a time in the Grub when my fear was so intense, it was beyond words. We heard German soldiers walking nearby, talking in German as they passed by the cowshed. The dog with them began to bark, and sniffing and scratching around the stable. We were so terrified, that I think we stopped breathing; we knew that at any moment we could be discovered. We heard the Nazis calling and whistling to the dog, and the dog left the stable. Apparently, the Germans did not think that there could be anyone hiding under the stable floor, so we were saved from discovery. The immediate danger and fear abated, leaving behind the "normal fear and the endless hunger."

James Hillman, in his book *The Dream and the Underworld* states, "heaven and hell are in our lives here and now, in this world; they are not coming in the next world."

The Holocaust experience was pure hell, and the terrorist attacks on the Twin Towers and the Pentagon were also hell: a living hell, and a continuous nightmare.

The heavenly moments that Hillman spoke of, if and when they come, are brief like lightning. We have to open ourselves up to them, and remember them when we find ourselves in hell.

Please write soon.
Yours,
Rita

16th September 2001

Yesterday, I finally managed to reach my sister in Manhattan. We had a good talk and I felt close to her in this time of catastrophe, tragedy and mourning. We know that our enemies will find ways to blame us for what happened. Everybody hates the Jews. My sister told me that she had already felt some hostility from one of her neighbors who, till the attacks on September 11, had been friendly with her.

I remember the suicide attack on the Dolphinarium in Tel Aviv: young people dancing and enjoying themselves, when suddenly, their bodies were blasted all over the entrance to the nightclub. My apartment is quite near the Dolphinarium, but I did not hear the blast because I was watching a movie on television. I heard a lot of sirens wailing and my suspicion was aroused. So I tuned in to watch the news channel and saw the catastrophe.

Tears and heartache, a familiar feeling these days, came over me. At moments like these, you stay close to the television, even though you know that the horror of the images will become indelible in your memory. The feelings are made worse by the fact that there is nothing you can do to stop the slaughter. Still, I am afraid to turn the TV and radio off, as if by keeping the news on, I can stop anything more from happening.

Today, I am sitting in a coffee shop, called Proza (Prose), which was recommended to me by a friend. I love the atmosphere here, because the coffee shop is also a bookshop. Books of all different kinds, mostly in Hebrew, surround me. I had seen enough of the ruins in Manhattan and needed a break. The horror and extent of this tragedy boggle the mind. When I saw the images of the people crying out for help and jumping from the windows, I wondered what, in their doom, they were thinking.

I remember being in the Grub when I was around eight years old, planning my own death by suicide. I just could not bear to live like that anymore: the stench, the fear, the hunger, a living nightmare. I remember that my mother was angry with me, although I cannot recall the reason. I cried, and then made the decision to kill myself. When the revolting "mush" was sent down to us, I refused to eat any, thinking that if I stopped eating, then I would die. My next idea was to run out of the Grub so that the Germans would see me and kill me. But I realized that if I did this, our hiding place would be discovered and my family would also die.

I then devised another plan. I waited one night until my father went out to find or steal some food. I know that he risked his life each time he did this, but he did not want us to starve. I waited until he had left and everyone else was sleeping and then I took the small pair of scissors that my mother used for sewing and cutting our hair. I cut off all the buttons from our clothes – shmattes by then – rags. I then swallowed all the buttons, counting each as it went down. My mother used to teach us in the Grub, whispering things to us such as *Yiddishe Lieder*, Jewish songs, and math. So I practiced my math by counting each button I swallowed, hoping that by swallowing enough, they would kill me.

I waited for death to come, but instead had a horrific stomachache. I tried to conceal the sharp pains, but could not stifle my moans. My mother must have heard and realized that something was wrong with me. Eventually, she managed to get the whole story out of me, as the pain became sharper and more intense. She immediately went up to see the farmer's wife and brought back a cup of pig's fat for me to drink. When the drink began to work, I had terrible diarrhea and all the buttons came out. Because I had counted the buttons as I they went in, I was able to tell my mother exactly how many there were, and she counted them again on the way out, to make sure I passed them all.

When my father returned, my hunger pangs were so intense that I could not resist, and ate from what he had brought. So life continued in the Grub, a living death. No respite came from the nightmare until the liberation.

21st September 2001

This morning, I rushed out to the coffeehouse across the street to write in my diary. At home, I find it difficult to concentrate; I either want to sleep or watch the news. Recently, I have been semi-comatose, half-asleep.

Ever since the terrorist attacks on the United States, I have been either glued to the television, flicking from CNN to Israeli channels, listening to Kol Yisrael on the radio, or sleeping. I have very little energy; I am functioning at a minimal level. Maybe if I drink some coffee it will wake me up, since I have decided to be awake now. The entries that I have made in my diary in the last three months are collectively called "Awake." But even drinking coffee in my favorite coffeehouses does not help much; it only gives me acid in my stomach. I am in a sleepwalking mode; I want to close my eyes most of the time.

I guess that I want to close my eyes to the terror that seems to engulf me: in Israel, New York, and Washington, all over the world.

How much more terror will my eyes have to witness? I cannot bear it anymore, but I cannot distance myself or become indifferent to the murder of thousands of innocents. They say that over six thousand people are buried in the rubble of what was the World Trade Center; bodies buried under steel and dust. The victims' loved ones will carry pain in their hearts forever: they cannot even bury their dead, nor will many be able to when the rubble is cleared. Those who are "lucky" will find only bits of their loved ones, identified by DNA.

What about the six million Jewish people who perished in the Holocaust? There weren't many left alive to mourn for loved ones lost. Only a handful of survivors, and those who had escaped to safe countries before the war began. The extermination camps left no traces of the victims that had been led to the slaughter within their walls. Six million Jews erased from existence and all that remained were the ashes from the gas chambers!!

I remember that I closed my eyes most of the day and night while we lived, or rather, endured, in the Grub. There was hardly any light in our hole; I could barely see when my eyes were open during the daytime. Living that way was like living in a heavy fog; at night we were in total darkness – pitch black. I found things to do during those dark and empty days. I would close my eyes and try to daydream: to dream was to escape the Grub. I would scrape mud from the walls of the Grub with my little hands. I found that the damp, mud walls were pliable like clay. I created little teacups, saucers, and teapots from the mud, fantasizing about having tea parties with friends. In my fantasy, my friends and I wore pink crinoline dresses, and ate small sweet cakes that my mother had baked.

My mother was a great baker. When she was orphaned at the age of eight, she moved in with a family that owned a bakery in Vilna and worked there until she married my father. She was like a daughter to the family; she enjoyed all the cultural events that Vilna had to offer at that time.

24*th* September 2001

I am staying at my son's house in Salit; it is about twenty minutes from Kfar Saba. My grandchildren have left for school. I am taking care of them for a few days while my son and his wife are away. My grandchildren left in high spirits, smiling and waving goodbye. They are so beautiful. They know their routine: they get up and brush their teeth, eat their favorite breakfast cereal, any variety they choose – whatever their heart's desire. They get dressed in nice clothes with famous labels on their backpacks: Pokemon, Digimon, etc. A bus picks them up and brings them home. They have their favorite friends, their favorite teachers and their favorite subjects. Some subjects they may like less, or even not at all, but they are accustomed to their routine. They come home after school to eat whatever food they choose for lunch. They each have their own room, filled with the best toys and equipment that money can buy: computers, television, and videos. They participate in many activities: swimming, sports, and trips to friends and family on ski vacations.

What was my routine at that age? What did I do when I was the age of my youngest grandchild? I got up, either in the morning or during the night; it did not matter in the Grub. The first feeling was always hunger, and then there was the problem of going to the bathroom. I hated to decide whether or not to face the horrible stench of the hole in the floor that was our toilet, the bullfrogs that were covered in excrement, or to stay where I lay and pee on the straw beneath me. If I urinated on the straw, I would have to lie there in my own filth. I would try to go back to sleep, to escape from the hunger and everything else.

When I was not sleeping, I would sit in my tunnel with my legs just outside, swaying backward and forward for hours and hours on end. When my mother was awake, I would sit beside her and whisper the numbers that she had taught me or sing in whispers the *Yiddishe* songs. Eventually, some mush would come down and we would eat it, though it was probably inedible. Thankfully, I cannot remember how it tasted. I would then start scraping the walls with my fingers to get some clay to make my tea set. I would imagine the wonderful cookies that my mother had baked. We were drinking tea, my friends and I, all wearing our pretty pink crinoline dresses.

I am not sure whether I ever drank tea or held tea parties wearing pretty dresses before the war. I don't know why I imagined tea and not hot chocolate. But I do know that I ate cookies – when I began my hunger strike that was all I would eat.

We stayed in the Grub for nineteen months and five days.

My father was always in contact with the farmer and, in this way, we were kept up-to-date on all the developments of the war and the battles between the Germans and the Russians. He heard that the front line was moving closer and closer to our hiding place.

WE LEAVE THE GRUB

One night, my father decided that it was too dangerous to remain in the Grub. He thought that our only chance was to cross the battle zone to the Russian front line. We climbed out of the Grub into the starry night, which had remained hidden from us for so long. My sister, crippled from being cramped in the Grub for so long, could not walk, so my father took an empty sack from the farm and made two holes in it. Then, he put her and my brother inside the sack so that their heads stuck through the holes and he carried them away from the Grub. I couldn't walk at first, but I could crawl. My mother walked unsteadily, guiding me by the hand in the same manner as one would walk a dog on a leash.

The first thing I remember seeing were the stars and the moon over me. They looked awesome to me, far up in the vast sky. We crossed over a cornfield, the corn pricking my skin as I crawled through it. I don't remember how long it took us to cross the cornfield, but I remember that when we came out, we heard shots, echoed by more and more shots. I assume that we were in a battle zone, caught in the crossfire between the Germans and the Russians.

It was still night time when we crossed over a second field. My father went ahead to figure out from which direction the bullets were coming. In this way, he would know which direction to take. Mother sat us all down next to a bush and put our heads together as we waited for our father to return. I think she did this because she figured that if a bomb were to fall on us, we would all die together. We were all very afraid; but it was a different kind of fear to what we had felt inside the Grub. In the Grub, the fear was in my mind, but this was different; this fear was solely in my body. My mind was blank, but I felt a great pressure in my chest, as if it were on fire. It was not like heartburn; it was something different, but it burned. We became increasingly afraid for my father as the minutes passed by and the bombs began to fall all around us.

All of a sudden, we heard a loud sigh and the sound of something falling to the ground with a thump, and then silence. We thought that my father had been hit. Mother ran in the direction of the sound and I followed her with my two younger siblings crawling behind me. I strained my eyes to search the darkness that surrounded me, though my eyes were used to the darkness of the Grub. I saw a white horse with gray patches lying dead on the ground; it had been shot. I looked up and saw a shadow moving toward us in the darkness. I knew it was my father even before he called out "Musia! Musia, *dos bin ich* (it's me)." As I was looking toward my father, I heard a loud explosion behind me. Turning around, I saw that the bush we had been sitting next to only moments ago was on fire. As I looked at the burning bush, the flames licking its branches and leaves, I felt the burning sensation in my chest disappear as though it had suddenly burnt itself out. A heavy weight had been lifted from my chest. I felt light, almost giddy, as we hugged and kissed our father on a battlefield in the middle of the night, with the stars and moon shining down on us.

The sight of the burning bush symbolized something to me, but what? Was it a miracle that I had survived when every second was fraught with danger? After the liberation, I continuously ruminated, "Why did I survive while six million others perished? Why did I survive and Anne Frank did not?"

We headed for the woods. My father gathered my sister and brother in his arms and placed them once more in the sack. Mother and I followed him, walking together, hand in hand. By this stage, I somehow miraculously was able to walk. Once we reached the forest, I lay down on the damp moss, gazing at the tall trees silhouetted above me, breathing in deeply the fresh air. The gunfire stopped, the woods became eerily quite, almost tranquil. I felt the fresh air cleanse my nostrils as I inhaled – at last I was free of the stench of the Grub. As I lay on the moss, about to fall asleep, I had a moment of insight, of truth – I don't know what to call it. I remember knowing with a clear certainty that I would never again experience such an extreme level of fear, fear of an imminent death that is impossible to bear.

25th *September 2001*

My grandson came into my bedroom to wake me this morning. He is so friendly and loving. He has a cough, but would not allow me to give him any medicine. He said that I had already tricked him into taking the worst medicine in the world. He said that I had told him that it tasted like honey but it didn't and it was awful! He made the appropriate facial expressions to make sure that he had made his point clearly. I knew that no amount of coaxing would make him change his mind and take the medicine. He gritted his teeth, in effect locking them to all horrible tasting liquids, and that was the end of that! He is such a beautiful child, and smart too. I love my grandchildren very much; they are so precious. I feel sad every time we part; it is hard, especially with the youngest child, Yair, who always argues with me to stay longer. He says that it is "not true" that I have to leave. I feel a twinge of guilt every time I leave him.

I got out of bed and went to the kitchen to make sandwiches for the children. After a quick breakfast, they left to take the bus to school. I sat down for a moment to plan what to make for lunch.

What a pleasant way to wake up in the morning, surrounded by beautiful and loving grandchildren. I gaze out of the kitchen window into my son and daughter-in-law's beautiful garden. I see the sun shining and feel the fresh warm breath of the morning air. I can hear the birds chirping merrily in the trees; it stirs my memory. As I look out the window, it strikes me again how wonderful the view is, with the flowers and trees blooming in harmony, in a burst of color and light. From this window, I can see the Arab villages in the surrounding area; on a clear day it is possible to see the sea in the distance.

The house is hushed after all the hustle and bustle of the children as they prepared to go to school. They have two beautiful cats, one that is beige with long hair and green eyes, and the other, pure white. The cats are sleeping now, one on the dining room table and the other on the couch. I fed them some chicken for breakfast, which, along with the peaceful atmosphere of the house, lulled them to sleep.

A memory comes to me of my waking, the night we left the Grub and crossed the battle zone through no-man's land to the Russian front line. It must have been summer, although I cannot remember what month it was. I awoke in a forest on a bed of soft moss to the sound of birds chirping around me. I opened my eyes and saw rays of sunlight peeping through the tall trees above me. At that moment, a kind of joy filled my heart. The moment was miraculous: waking up bathed in sunlight after almost two years in total darkness. I looked and looked at the patterns that the sun cast onto the leaves in the trees above me; the leaves sparkled as they basked in the natural beauty of the sunshine. I inhaled the fresh air and smelled the wonderful scent of the moss underneath me; it was the most marvelous smell I had ever experienced.

I remember the feeling of complete elation, as I lay in the glade and listened to the birds' song. I wanted to sing and dance, but most of all, I wanted to live. The natural beauty of the life that surrounded me filled me such an intense will to live, to live like a bird or the tiny caterpillar that crawled on the tree beside me. I wanted to roam in the fields and woods like the gypsies who wandered from place to place in the stories that my mother had whispered to me in the Grub.

I remember the joyful moments from my childhood so vividly. I remember rolling on the straw that had been scattered on the floor for the Passover Seder. I was wearing a new pair of black patent leather shoes. The straw smelled so fresh. Then I remembered the straw in the Grub. The stench of that straw that I lay on, slept on, urinated on and sat on as I made my tea sets from mud with my little hands.

28th *September 2001*

The sun is setting on the beach next to Frishman Street. It is a fabulous sight: a huge red burning ball hanging over the sea sinking slowly beyond the horizon, casting fiery colors in its wake. Its magnetic power compels me to stare at it and meditate until it disappears into oblivion. Soon, night will fall and the atmosphere will be changed and filled with night sounds: the sky filled with stars reflecting their heavenly light on the ominously dark ocean, dark and deep with its own secrets.

Jung compared the ocean to the unconscious mind, which incorporates all of our processes: evolutionary, cultural, and psychological. And of course, the processes of repression, as described by Freud: the kind of secrets that are expressed in dreams, which we attempt to interpret symbolically and not always with success. Jung attempted to reach to his own fountain of knowledge. There were many times when he felt that he was going overboard and losing contact with reality. He needed to assure himself that he was Carl Jung, here and now: I live in… I am married to… etc.

Yesterday (September 26 and 27) was Yom Kippur. I fasted and went to the synagogue next to my house to pray. I prayed a lot; I always do on Yom Kippur. I prayed the Yizkor, which is a remembrance prayer. I prayed for my parents who are gone now, and for all the members of my family who were murdered by the Nazis during the Holocaust; I do this every year. When I returned from the synagogue after praying Kol Nidrei, I went to sleep. This year, on the night of Yom Kippur, I dreamt a lot. Maybe it was because I fasted and slept. They were strange dreams; I don't know how to connect them to my life.

29*th* September

Dear Rita,

I wish you a happy New Year and all the best for the future; I hope all your dreams come true.

I am sorry to hear that you have been depressed lately; you seemed to be feeling a bit more hopeful, what with the opportunity to make a film of your Holocaust experience. I understand that things have become stuck, because you had to let the photographer go: he must have really pressed the wrong buttons with you for you to feel you had to end your association with him. Try not to let yourself become too disheartened, though; you have other creative things to do, such as your writing and painting.

I am always amazed at how well you seem to remember all the events of your tumultuous history, including the very painful and traumatic aspects of your Holocaust experience.

I am also amazed that you still remember me. It has been many years since you regularly corresponded with me, and it was 1984 when you first dreamt of me. You were at a crossroads in your life then, trying to decide whether to leave Israel for San Francisco.

You told me that your friends tell you that your memory amazes them, that you can recall aspects of their personal history that they themselves have forgotten.

Keep working on becoming more conscious, what you call being awake. Wake up, Rita! Get out of the Grub. Concentrate on being awake and don't sleep away your days hiding from everyone. You have to become more active; try not to procrastinate like you have in the past.

Yours,
Jay

THE MARCH TO FREEDOM

1st October 2001

I am really trying to become more awake: to have an awakening. I hope to persevere with my decision to become more active and to avoid a relapse of reverting to my old and now well-worn techniques of survival. I have found that taking walks along the beach helps.

The semester begins at the university in about three weeks, and I have not even begun to prepare. "I will survive it all" is my motto, but what about not just surviving things, but actually living my life? Do I create the situations in which I feel I need to survive? Do I prevent myself from really living? Perhaps, by merely surviving the reality of my life here and now, I feel less guilty about surviving when six million others perished.

Enough of this analysis; back to nature I think – with some meditation, walking and fresh air, I will overcome my lethargy.

I have always had trouble with writing: my grammar, vocabulary and sentence structure leave a lot to be desired. Where could I have learned structure during my formative years? It couldn't be the Grub or in the displaced persons camps. I started regular schooling at high school age in the United States. I taught myself Yiddish after learning the alphabet. Throughout my studies, I have always had marks deducted for writing errors. I was never able to take notes, so I copied from other students and avoided writing letters as much as possible, usually with the excuse that my family did not write to each other; we spoke on the phone. My writing incapacity caused me the greatest problems when I worked as a social worker for the Jewish Agency for Immigrants, when I had to write reports in Hebrew. I really suffered when I had to write up intakes and reports on the patients I had treated. When I worked as an art therapist in a psychiatric ward, I agonized over every document that I had to submit.

It is strange, I suppose, but now I want to write all the time. My writing skills have improved, but I feel that time is running out for me; I need to march forward with my writing. I feel that I have a lot to tell the world. I don't want to die, taking that knowledge with me.

I took a walk along the beach on Saturday afternoon and the scene, as evening approached, was so wonderful that it is hard to describe. As I was walking (marching!), the sun was setting, and clouds scattered in the vast, darkening expanse of sky. A cloud obscured the sinking sun, which looked as though it had shattered into pieces of fire falling into the horizon beyond. The sea was

The "Grub" (The Pit), Photographer, Dr. Zeev Hertz Folman

The Bloody Train 2 – 2010, Photographer, Dr. Zeev Hertz Folman

The Bloody Train – 2006

The Nazi Murder Machine 2 – 2006

Maidanek – 2006

Massacre at Gura – 350 children were murdered – 2006

Shooting – Murdering in Poland – 2005

March to Freedom – 2005

Before the Wedding – 2009

Waiting for the Rabbi – 2009, Photographer, Dr. Zeev Hertz Folman

Before the Honeymoon – 2009

Romantic Venice – 2009, Photographer, Dr. Zeev Hertz Folman

threatening, its huge waves frothing powerfully as they crashed onto the sand. Hues of peach and opal spread between the floating clouds, becoming darker with the setting sun. Now, the sea became the darkest blue, nearing black; the dark expanse of water was broken only by the foaming waves reaching the shore. The air was wonderfully fresh and the water beneath my feet was warm and pleasant. The moon had already ascended without waiting for the sun to disappear; she now became the queen of the night, the stars accompanying her in procession on their endless journey. These moments, when I am in awe of the wonders of nature, I feel such a strong desire to live life to its fullest – strange, then, that I should also think of death.

In *The Oxford Book of Death*, Montague writes, "Let us deprive death of its strangeness, let us frequent it, let us get used to it, let us have nothing more often in our minds than death.... We do not know where death awaits us: so let us wait for it everywhere. To practice death is to practice freedom." While walking, I pondered over the books I have recently read. A lot of the material is from Buddhist teachings and it contains some interesting approaches to death.

11th October 2001

It has been ten days since I last wrote an entry in my diary: holidays, family, dinners, lunches – time flies. I am going away to a retreat soon, to practice meditation instead of procrastination. I feel so off-center and scattered; perhaps a weekend there will relax and center me. I am on the move, though; I have woken up somehow, marching on, on the run, march to the end – I still need to publish my diaries; I have so much to do before the final exit.

14th October 2001

I came back from the weekend retreat yesterday evening. The retreat did wonders for me; it helped me feel more centered.

I was with a group that practiced an offshoot of Zen philosophy. We stayed at a kibbutz near Jerusalem, where we meditated and slowed ourselves down completely; we walked slowly and had a lot time to think and reflect. We practiced "Royal Silence," deep listening, and mindfulness. We learned how to meditate while walking, which I found very calming.

The leader of the group gave me feedback; he said that I was very open and active and that I adapted easily to new things. I remember that a supervisor, with whom I worked in the past, had told me that if I were dropped in the North Pole, I would have no problem learning how to build myself an igloo! The leader of the group said that he felt as though I had been with them for awhile, which was flattering, as this was my first time on this kibbutz where we both led groups.

I felt very free to express myself there, although there was one instance when I felt that my views were not received well. I sang a prayer, "Al Naharot Bavel," a psalm which has become associated with Zionism. While I sang, I noticed that the group did not sing along with me, as I'd expected they would. I understand that Sanga teachings and theories are universal, centered on all nations sharing awareness and interacting with one another. While I believe in peace, I also believe that it is difficult understanding and interact with people that terrorize and persecute our nation. I wanted to sing this prayer, so I did; contrary to what the leader had said to me, I was neither able nor willing to accept their views: I am a Zionist, I am an Israeli, and I am Jewish. The majority of the group was Jewish, although there were a few Arabs present.

The Zen philosophy teaches the principles of nonviolence: to show compassion to even the most violent terrorists. I know that the Zen group was trying to encourage more Arab members, and by singing a Zionist prayer from the Bible, I went counter to their ideas.

After lunch, we visited a nearby Arab village with the intention of talking about peace. We did not smoke a peace pipe, but we did drink very black, very bitter coffee together.

I especially enjoyed the walks and the atmosphere, the stillness and quiet of meditating while walking – walking so slowly that I could almost fall asleep. I felt a profound liberation in letting go, being free, and slowing down. I connected with the method and felt that it allowed a person to gain inner knowledge.

We walked in circles and lines, wandering freely around the kibbutz, enjoying the spectacular scenery. We were taught to walk very slowly; we were to take two steps and then fix our gaze on a different point in the natural beauty that surrounded us, and then to take another two steps. Even now I can visualize some of the perfect picture postcard sites lodged in my memory from the walks. We mostly concentrated on our breathing and increased our awareness of our surroundings and learning to be aware of every moment.

I was with a friend from Jerusalem and we talked and enjoyed ourselves. Sometimes the "Royal Silences" interfered with our conversation, but I suppose we were, at times, gabbing too much. The silences were good for us: to not feel compelled to be nice and polite to everyone, to not feel the need to stick to the good manners we have been taught. I was free to pass people by without interaction, smiling only at those I felt like smiling at. There was no need to make polite conversations with strangers.

Still, that night I had a terrible dream, which I cannot shake off. It is too difficult for me at this moment to describe it owing to the fear it invokes within me. I have decided to write it down later. I hope I won't forget, but maybe I will.

According to Zen, love is to merge with the universe embracing all, even the tiniest of insects. The leader asked us what our perceptions of love were. There were some members in the group who said it was an obsession, others who said that it was the love of children, tolerance, forgiveness, compassion and a feeling of melting with the universe. I sang a song:

> Love on a high and wintry hill,
> In the morning mist,
> When two lovers kissed,
> And the world stood still.
> Love is nature's way of giving
> A reason for believing,
> For giving and receiving....

What is love to me? It is ecstasy, passion and turmoil. Love, in all its consuming forms, has existed throughout the ages and yet its essence still eludes us. Plato compared love to the appreciation of beauty, but what is beautiful? "Beauty is in the eye of the beholder." Shakespeare, I think, said it best, when he famously asked, "What is love?" and then left the question unanswered.

21st October 2001

Today, I received a letter from one of my former patients, telling me that she is about to get married. It was a beautiful letter; in it she thanked me for giving her new hope. She said that her heart is now filled with love, happiness and appreciation for the healing process she went through with me. I never expect my patients to be so demonstrative of their appreciation, and when someone takes the time to tell me that I have helped them and that they are grateful, it touches me deeply. I experience the same thing when someone is kind to me; I am profoundly touched and sometimes moved to tears.

I will let the analysts figure that one out. At this point, I am so tired of analyzing myself, doing everything for myself. I would like someone to take care of me.

An ex-boyfriend re-emerged into my life recently – probably, as is usually the case, for a brief episode, since we are not suited to one another. He comes back, usually after a divorce or failed relationship, and we pick up where we left off, but then we part again, no doubt to come together again and again in the future.

A memory from the war years appears in my mind. I am lying

in the woods inhaling the fresh air and smell of the moss that surrounds me, filling my nostrils. I can see the sun slowly setting as I look up through the tall trees. I remember the desire to remain suspended in that moment forever; at that moment, I felt that the beauty of my surroundings could hold me there happily. I wanted only to absorb the smells that wafted around me, the fluttering of the birds, chirping away above me. What fantastic greenery encircled me! I stood up and hugged one of the trees; I wanted so much to live and be a part of the beauty all around me. As I stood resting my head on the tree, my heart brimmed with love for the world. I gazed at everything with amazement: the birds chirping up in the trees, the mushrooms growing at my feet, the caterpillar crawling near my head on a branch of the tree. I felt light-headed. I find it difficult to communicate the intensity of that moment, the way I felt it all those years ago. I can still vividly recollect how wonderful everything appeared to me then: simply having the space to stand up filled me with wonder after the months of near-immobility in the darkness of the Grub.

Suddenly, I heard a shot. It echoed around me in the stillness of the glade. I was shattered and sat up shocked on the shuddering earth. The birds took to the air in fright and flew away, no doubt in search of peace and tranquility. The battle between the Russians and Germans had resumed, and once more, we were caught in the middle. The noise of the gunfire echoed all around us incessantly for what seemed to me an eternity; sometimes it seemed quite distant, and other times it was very close.

My family and I lay quiet and still in the forest glade until the gunfire ceased. My father told us that we would have to start moving again, this time in the direction of Turmont where our house was situated. Somehow, we had to cross over to the Russian side. He said that was our only hope of survival – in truth, our saviors would have to be the Russians.

We began to trek into the darkness, toward our only hope. My father knew his way very well and was able to guide us easily.

We walked for days, hiding during daylight and walking by night. My father still carried my brother and sister in the sack while my mother and I followed behind. This was our strangely surreal march to freedom, marching to the Russian front line.

During our march, we saw no other living soul. It seemed that everybody had left, abandoning their houses and possessions in their haste to escape from the battle. Occasionally, we came across dead animals that had fallen victim to the gunfire. Miraculously, we were left unscathed, as we picked our route through no-man's land. The German and Russian bullets missed us – every second was a miracle.

I remember stopping at houses and peering through the broken windows. We found food in those houses. Apparently, the occupants had left in such a hurry that they had left food laid out and ready to eat on the table.

29*th* October 2001

Today is a day of remembrance and mourning for a great leader, Yitzchak Rabin, who was shot dead by a young Jewish man after speaking to a large crowd in Tel Aviv about peace with the Arabs for our nation. In 1995, with thousands of Israelis, I mourned in the square, renamed Rabin Square. Despite the sadness, there was also a sense of togetherness with my fellow mourners: united in a feeling of sorrow and hope.

I live only a few streets away from Rabin Square, but this year I did not attend the memorial, watching it on television instead. I am still too overloaded with sadness and regret and did not want to cry anymore. How much trauma, mourning and sadness can a person take? My heart is cruelly ripped out every time there is a terrorist attack or another news bulletin bearing tidings of nothing but woe. Yesterday, there was a shooting: four dead and thirty-five injured, some of them seriously. Each time I turn on the television, my home is invaded with images of sorrow, death and innocent bloodshed. Men, women and children – none are spared, none are safe.

I want to scream out to God and the universe, when will it all end? Didn't I and millions of others already suffer enough? I survived the hell of the Holocaust. Wasn't that enough to fill my quota of misery and pain? Of course, I get no answer from anybody, just a lot of words that don't make any sense to me. There is so much confusion here; it makes me feel sleepy.

I promised that I would stay awake and continue marching until the end. At this moment, all I want to do is go to sleep and leave this sorry mess behind. But I keep my body glued to the chair and continue to write my diary. Perhaps it is my fate to continuously search for meanings in the mysteries of life and death.

I remember another time when the specter of death was imminent. After scavenging food from the deserted houses, with their sad, broken windows, we continued on our trek toward the Russian frontline. We continued our strange procession for days, although I am not sure how many. One night, we came to a lake that my father said we needed to cross, as it was the safest way back to Turmont and to our home. He said that if we went across the lake, we would avoid the gunfire, and that he knew the shallowest places.

My mother cried and said that she couldn't do it. She pleaded with my father, "Please, Nochim, you must leave us now. You go alone and save yourself; so that you at least will live. We cannot make it together." My father would not listen for one moment to my mother's protests. He said that there was no way that he would leave us there to die and save only himself. My father then took my mother to one side and they whispered together so that we could not hear.

We began the march into the shallow part of the lake where there was probably a crossing to the other side, wading through the waters. I don't remember how we got onto a boat in the night's darkness, but my father rowed for approximately nine miles on the lake. As morning came, we arrived at a small, pebbled clearing out of which a road led. On that road, I remember noticing tank tracks. From these tracks, I concluded that our messiah was near and I fell on my knees to bow and kissed the tanks' imprints. As I looked up, I noticed Russian soldiers ahead of us standing by their tanks.

Just for a moment, try to envisage the scene of my family walking along in our strange procession. My head was shorn and I still wore that filthy nightgown made of coarse linen. My mother was all red; the red outfit she had knitted for herself in the Grub had run from the wool and colored her skin. My father was the only member of our group that looked anywhere near normal, aside from the hunchback formed by two young children, whose heads were also shorn, sticking out from a sack on his back.

The Russian soldiers stood by the tanks staring at us. Some of the soldiers made the sign of the cross. They did not utter a word; they let us pass without taking their eyes off us for a moment. They acted as if they were seeing ghosts: a family of ghosts, walking toward them from the grave.

HOME SWEET HOME

28th November 2001

I particularly love one special room in my home. A Russian artist friend of mine decorated it in the style of a Japanese garden and it has become my sanctuary. The tables and chairs, made of genuine wood, combined with the artwork, make a serene and peaceful retreat. This is where I go to meditate, and where my patients come for therapy sessions. Many tales from other people's lives – hopes, dreams and concerns – have crossed this simple wooden table, which I lean on to write now.

As I sit in this oasis of calm from the bustling life of Tel Aviv, a memory comes to me from another time in another home. When the Germans invaded Poland, they torched our original home in Dryswiaty and relocated us to the ghetto. After my family and I completed our perilous journey through no-man's land to the Russian front line, we headed for our other home in Turmont, where my father's business had been located.

I was too young at that time and, more than likely, too traumatized, to have any expectations of what our homecoming would be like. We found the house totally empty; the Germans had used it as a headquarters. They had literally occupied our house as well as our country. They left nothing behind them – everything was stripped bare. What had formerly been our home and my father's business was now an empty shell; wooden floorboards and bare walls were all that remained. We came home to a house stripped bare by an army of men who had demolished everything we had possessed. They did not simply invade our country; they invaded families and communities, which, with deadly planned precision, they swiftly ripped apart. In short, anything that was of significance to us was destroyed. They tried to rid the world of us. They tried to obliterate our faith and our identity. In contrast to love, security, and life, they left hatred, desolation and death.

From left: my little brother, father, mother, me, friends, and sister, Turmont, Poland, 1946

Everything was so quiet and empty in Turmont. We were ghosts, raised from the grave, returning to our ghost house in a ghost town that had previously been so full of life. I remember how the floorboards creaked as we walked over them, proving that we were, in fact, alive. Russian soldiers came to give us some food. The scrambled eggs tasted indescribably wonderful, as if I were eating for the first time.

At that time, things were so unreal that I cannot recall the exact sequence of events. I remember my father telling us that he had been drafted into the Russian army and that he was going to see if there was anything he could do about it. Once again, my mother, brother, sister and I sat in a circle, this time on our bare wooden floorboards, with our heads together, and cried bitterly. We were lost again. The danger had not passed; it seemed we were going to be without a father. Three or four hours passed, maybe more, until father returned and told us that he had fixed things so that he wouldn't have to join the army. Then, we all cried again; we cried for our suffering and that of countless others, but we also cried from relief and happiness that the worst appeared to be over, that we had survived hell and were sitting here in our home together.

Many months passed, of which I have no recollection. No one I ever knew as a child was still alive. They had killed my grandmothers, all my uncles except for one, aunts, and cousins, as well as all those girls I had imagined having tea parties with. When we came home, no one, no one from our town had survived. We were the only ones left as a nuclear family. We survived only thanks to my father, who was a *very great hero*, and whose resourcefulness and love for his family inspired his heroic acts to keep us alive together.

A Jewish organization located us and we began our journey from Poland. We traveled to Germany, to the town of Ulm, and later to the displaced persons camp in Bad Reichenhall.

1st December 2001

I was sitting in a coffee shop in Tel Aviv waiting for a friend. The coffee shop, called Tom, was recommended to me by the producer of the documentary film that I plan to make. Recently, we haven't made any progress with the project, but I am not totally disheartened, as the draft of my manuscript is almost finished. My friend was late, which was unusual for her, so I made the best use of my time by writing in my diary. After she arrived and we had lunch together, we went to the opera. My friend is a very intelligent and cultured woman; she has always been interested in my Holocaust experience, her family having immigrated to Israel from Berlin before the war.

The coffeehouse was alive with hustle and bustle, full of young people eating lunch, talking and laughing loudly to each other or into their cell phones, and smoking like chimneys, so that I had to switch tables three times. All the same, I liked the atmosphere there: young Israelis enjoying themselves on a Saturday afternoon, laughing, joking, and smoking so much, even though the threat of a terrorist attack is possible at any time.

My friend told me about a friend of hers who had had an experience in Poland just after the war, in which they had suffered at the hands of the Polish people. During the war, many Poles actively collaborated with the Nazis. There was a film released recently called *Neighbors*, which dealt with this subject.

Our discussion reminded me of a time many years ago when my family and I traveled from Poland to Germany, and I became very ill with a high fever. My family got off the train and took me to a hospital in a small Polish town. The doctors could not diagnose what was wrong with me (many years later, after analyzing my symptoms, I discovered that my illness was most probably an acute reaction to trauma). My temperature was so high that I almost died. I was in the hospital for three or four weeks, during which my father secured good treatment for me, by giving the doctors gifts of cigarettes and other goodies. While I was in the hospital, my family stayed in a small house on the outskirts of the town. The small house was very basic; it didn't even have a stove to cook on. My family built small fires outside to cook their meals. One night, while they were thus cooking their dinner outside, some Polish people began shooting at them. By some miracle, nobody in my family was shot. After that night, they went into hiding again, until I was released from the hospital.

My father was a very practical man with an indestructible will to survive. He decided that the best thing to do in order to provide for his family was to buy a horse and a cow: a horse, so he might earn a living, and a cow, so that we would not go hungry. However, now that we had a horse and cow, it was impossible to travel on a regular train, so we had to take one that transported livestock. I remember that one night on our journey, the train stopped at a junction near a train station. In the middle of the night, some Polish men attempted to break into our compartment. They almost succeeded in breaking down the door. We did not know whether they knew that we were there and why they had selected our compartment. Did they plan to steal our horse, our cow, or both? My father broke the window at the back of the compartment, and his younger brother, who was small enough to climb through, ran to get help. The police arrived just in time and took the Poles away.

4th December 2001

My son Alan called last night, concerned about me after all the terrible events of the weekend. He comforted me by telling me that the horrendous terrorist attacks that Israel continually suffers from cannot be compared to the Holocaust and that I should be careful, but not feel threatened as I did then. I assured him that I was feeling OK and that I always try to keep things in perspective about my experiences. I told him, "You can take me out of the Grub, but you can't take the Grub out of my memory, nor erase the scars it left in my heart." I will never forget the acute sense of blind terror and, try as I may, each time I watch the news and something terrible has happened, I am wounded again. I told my son that I don't forget anything and he laughed.

On Saturday evening, when I returned home from a wonderful day shared with a friend, I didn't turn on the radio or television, as I usually do. I relaxed, took a shower, and read for awhile. When I finally turned on the television, it was one o'clock in the morning. I had decided to watch the news bulletin before going to bed. I wish I hadn't. Horrible scenes from a terrorist attack in Jerusalem spilled out of my television screen and once again invaded my home with bloodshed and carnage. The scenes of explosions and people fleeing in terror looked like something from a horror movie. It was real, though: a hard, concrete reality. There is no hiding from it. I did not sleep that Saturday night. I wept and mourned for the innocents who had lost their lives while enjoying a coffee or a beer with friends. I cried for the grieving ones who are left in terror's wake.

On Sunday, I sat down to watch the news and saw that there had been another suicide bomb attack, on a bus in Haifa. Once again, in the span of just twelve hours, fear, horror, pain and rage rushed through my brain. A suicide bomber had boarded a bus, coolly paid his fare, walked to the middle, and detonated a bomb he had strapped to himself. The cold-blooded savageness of this action fills me with despair. In total, in just twelve short hours, twenty-five people lost their lives and around two hundred others were injured.

Sixty years ago, the world witnessed the evil that mankind is capable of committing against its own kind. Millions of people suffered and perished horrifically at the hands of their persecutors and for what? Have any lessons been learnt? Our lives were drowned in cruelty, hardship, suffering, and continuous hunger. Those who had survived the Holocaust nightmare prayed that they had endured enough and that the reward would be peace. How foolish! How naive! We are still the targeted victims to this day.

A mother takes a bus to pick up her son from school. She may be thinking about a course she wishes to study at college or perhaps what food to buy at the store. A fear exists in the back of her mind, a fear that lies dormant in the minds of all those who are threatened. She is not consciously aware of her fear. She thinks about her son. She will never be consciously aware of anything more from that moment onward. The bright flame of life that was burning is extinguished in a second. Nothing is left but the memory of her and the scars her death will leave on all those who loved her. That is terror. That is the result of terror. And this is just one fragment of the story, one person's life.

For those who survived, the images of those moments will be scorched on their brains: images of blood and burning flesh strewn about them. They will never forget the scene they witnessed that day: an ordinary day in Haifa, just as I will never forget the suffering I myself witnessed and endured. And now, for those that remain here, life must go on. Sometimes, it's difficult for me to remember why.

I will continue living. I will continue to enjoy the freedom that my country offers and fights to defend. I will continue to take buses and trains. If death stops me, so be it, I will die; it is inevitable. Everybody dies.

I am grateful for what I have now and for what I have accomplished. I have wonderful, intelligent, and successful children, and three amazing grandchildren. I am a writer, a teacher, and a painter. I have experienced the miracle of love. I have experienced the miracle of survival, when all around me was fraught with danger. For these things I am grateful to God. And if God grants me the time to do it, I plan to write two more books and two more plays.

5th December 2001

It is a cold, wet, and wintry day. The branches of my tree are swaying in the wind next to my window. Traveling up to Haifa is not a very inviting prospect, not because of the terrorist attacks, but because of the stormy weather.

The dull, gray weather transports me to another time, when my family and I traveled by train from Poland to Ulm, in Germany. It was as cold and wet as Polish weather can be. I don't know how many days or weeks we spent on the train, but it seemed to me a long time before we arrived at our destination. I don't recall anything about the town of Ulm, nor how long we stayed there. I do remember arriving in Bad Reichenhall, at the displaced persons camp. We had an apartment there, part of a compound set aside for Jewish Holocaust survivors, which we shared with one other family. I remember that I had to dress under the covers, as there was only a thin fabric partition separating our living area from the other family.

Rita's father and younger brother sitting on a motorcycle
in Bad Reichenhall, c. 1948

The compound had five or six buildings, each about six stories high. At the time, the buildings looked like skyscrapers to me. The camp was a kind of halfway house where displaced people stayed until they returned to their homes or emigrated. I found a life there that I liked. At that time, I was twelve years old and enjoyed being free to play and learn. There were many young people there for me to make friends with.

The few schoolteachers living in the camp, along with other educated people, divided us into groups and taught us everything they knew. We learned Hebrew, history and mathematics. We used to put on school plays, in which I thoroughly enjoyed acting. I became one of the better-known members of the class and the camp, as I played Queen Esther, a Hasid, and many other dancing and singing roles. I remember some of the songs that I sang were from *Aliyah Bet* in Yiddish from the book of Shmerke Kaczerginski. He was the author of *The Destruction of Vilna*, for which he interviewed my father and mother.

Rita was chosen to give the speech in Yiddish and Hebrew for
Israel's Declaration of Independence, Bad Reichenhall, 1948

While living in Bad Reichenhall, I belonged to a Zionist organization in which we learned about Israel and Zionism. In 1948, when Israel became independent, I gave a speech in Yiddish and Hebrew. There were many speeches made in celebration of an independent Jewish state, but I was the only child orator.

With my mother's help, I began to teach myself Yiddish even before the lessons had been organized. There was a small library, with books, such as Romain Rolland, Dostoevsky, and Tolstoy, which had been translated into Yiddish. I used to take a book from the library and go into the nearby woods to sit and read quietly by myself. I remember that my favorite books were the romantic ones. In retrospect, I see that I was drawn to the woods because I wanted to recapture the moment we escaped from the Grub into the woody glade; that was the moment I came back to life.

I made a lot of new friends in the camp, especially girlfriends. The children used to walk around the camp in lines, the girls usually at the front. Most of the girls were one or two years older than me, and I remember that they would quickly drop their conversation whenever I joined the group, which used to upset me. Later, I discovered that they had been talking about boys and kissing, and, because I was younger than they were, they didn't want me to hear.

I suppose they were right, because I was young and naive. My mother never discussed sex, or anything even remotely connected to reproduction with me. I remember when I got my first period: I didn't know why I was bleeding, and thought that something was wrong with me. I told my mother about the blood and she shouted to my father, "Nochim, Nochim, go and get the doctor!" My father hurriedly put on his boots and ran out of the door. My mother began to ask me questions, and in a matter of seconds, the cause of my "illness" was established. My mother ran to the door and called out, "Nochim, Nochim! Come back. Its alright."

Until that point, I had been a bit of a tomboy. I used to play soccer with the boys on the field. But then one day when I was playing, the cotton from my panties fell out as I kicked the ball and landed next to my feet covered in blood. I was terribly embarrassed and from that day onward, I never played soccer again.

Rita dancing the Hora with her friends, Bad Reichenhall, 1949

My first crush was on my math teacher. I can still picture him vividly, as if it were yesterday. He had dark, shining eyes and wore a gray flat cap and gray three-quarter-length woolen trousers. I used to lie in the woods reading romantic stories and thinking about him. I used to imagine that he would come into the woods, hold my hand, and be very impressed that I was reading such serious and deep books. I would also imagine that I was playing the piano in the school hall (we called it a hall but it was in fact only a room). He would come and sit beside me to listen, admiring me while I played.

I have always loved music. I remember telling my parents that I wanted to play the piano, so they sent me for lessons in a nearby town with an old German woman. I would sit and play the piano during these lessons and all of a sudden I would hear a thump: the old woman, who must have been about eighty-five, had fallen asleep and fallen from her chair in the process. I told my parents this and they stopped the lessons.

We lived in the camp, or *Lager*, as we called it, for three years between 1946 and 1949. During those years I had many happy times and made some good friends. In Bad Reichenhall, we learned how to live freely once more; we enjoyed our lives and were thankful that we had survived. In 1949, my father told us that we were going to leave Bad Reichenhall, Germany and Europe for a new life in the United States of America. We were going to take a boat across the ocean to New York, where we hoped to live happily ever after in the Land of the Free.

Rita singing, New York, 1951

Graduating high school, New York, 1952

Rita, mother of two, Boston, 1963

Rita's brother graduating college

Rita dining with her two children in Florida, c. 1967

EPILOGUE

A DREAM: A DIALOGUE WITH JAY

October 4th, 1996, the night before Yom Kippur (the Jewish Day of Judgment), I dreamt that I met a man, and that he would lead me to a special place.

I know that he is very spiritual and able to understand me. We meet next to a lake; he leads me over a bridge and into a forest. While we walk, I tell him about my Holocaust experience. It is very enjoyable to walk with him through the forest, surrounded by trees and many small bushes.

He is listening very attentively, but I sense that he does not understand some part of what I am saying. We sit down on the grass: he sits in front of me and spreads out some Tarot cards in a circle between us. They are not the usual variety of cards; they are covered with only black markings that may be Chinese symbols, but I am not sure. I don't know the meanings of these signs and cannot interpret the cards. He is looking at the cards. I look at him and the cards, but cannot recall what he looks like.

I look around me and I notice that the forest has many tall trees. As I am gazing at my surroundings, I catch sight of something in the trees that fills me with excitement and awe: a huge picture, like a wall painting or mural. It is a super-realistic picture and I can distinguish all the details. The picture stands among a group of small bushes, depicting a *yeshiva bocher* (student) with a thickly woven *talit* (prayer shawl) wrapped around him. The picture is very impressive; it seems almost panoramic.

I become frightened; fear creeps over my skin as I stare at the image of this picture. I cannot understand why the picture disturbs me so much. I cannot bear the intensity of my fear.

JAY: What do you understand about this dream? What does the vision of a *talit* mean to you?

RITA: This dream is a kind of prayer for me. It reminds me of the film *Dreams*, by Kurassow, which says that art is larger than life, and the art of van Gogh, which is panoramic in color and light. The *talit* symbolizes Judaism. This reminds me that I have to pray. I once went to a doctor in Israel who was a medical doctor, homeopath, and a *chozer biteshuva* (newly religious). He said that the solution to my chaotic life was to return to prayer and become religious, the best solution being to sit in a yeshiva and study the Torah. I did study Judaism for five years at the Jewish Theological Seminary in New York City, but I did not continue in this direction. I left this heritage to my brother, who continued very successfully in Judaism. In addition, the doctor said that I had to live with the Chabad Chasidim and give up the chaotic lifestyle that I am living now, wandering from one country to another, one episode to another. Perhaps the message is to move toward spirituality.

JAY: Do you miss the spiritual life of Judaism? Are you attracted to Judaism and spirituality, or are you afraid of it? Are you afraid of the *yeshiva bocher* and his *talit*? Are you afraid of praying? What are you afraid of? Does Judaism scare you?

RITA: After I finished at the Jewish Theological Seminary with a bachelor's degree in religious education, I seriously considered going for a doctorate. At the same time as I studied for my bachelor's in religious education, I was also studying for a bachelor of science degree at Columbia University. I completed both degrees in 1958. I am not afraid of Judaism; I practice my faith from the perspective of Conservative Judaism. After completing my degree, I didn't continue my studies in Judaism, but I did not lose any of my faith – nor did I lose the value of my faith, which to this day I would never relinquish. I suffered too much for my religion during the Holocaust to give it up.

And Judaism has been imprinted in my soul since my early childhood. My parents and my grandparents were always traditional Jews, especially my grandmother on my mother's side, who was extremely religious. My earliest memory of her is watching her praying most of the day by a small lamp. My dear grandmother, like most of my relatives, was brutally killed by the Nazi murder machine.

JAY: What is the message of the dream? What is the inner guide telling you? That this is a significant dream? That this dream is a sign of the soul and its meaning? Judaism has brought you a lot of tragedy; everything was taken away from you in the Holocaust. You were persecuted by the Nazis because you were Jewish, and you sacrificed everything that was healthy in your childhood. Your father, your mother, your whole family became victims of Nazi persecution. You and your family's suffering cannot be comprehended by ordinary people. You and your family had to give up your lives. You gave up all of the activities, connections and possessions. You had no home, no clothing, or food. You lived in continuous hunger and fear, and paid a terrible, heavy price for being Jewish. You left everything that you had invested in your studies of Judaism, probably with great conflict and heavy heart and therefore your life became a constant search for a place where you could feel safe and at home. You have never really found it. In your dream, the inner guide tells you look at the *talit*, look at the *yeshiva bocher*; it is larger than life. Look at your roots again and again; look at the history of your people, at the depth and length of that history and examine every detail of it.

And yet, you chose to make aliyah with your children and continue to live here to this day, where at long last you've found your home.

The inner truth is telling you about your roots. It is telling you that you have been running away from them. The images of the *yeshiva bocher* and the *talit* represent the history of your people; it is the deepest root that you have been running from. However, the question remains whether or not this is the answer; we cannot be sure. This is a special dream. Your inner world is very expressive. It seems that this dream was very clear and vivid for a purpose. Something spiritual will bring you to the right path. Something or someone spiritual will show you the secret, and therefore the significance, of this vision.

RITA: I feel that this guide understands me, but he does not understand, according to my perception, some things about the Holocaust.

JAY: But you were in some ways privileged to witness and experience a very intense event. We can look at the elements and images in your dream and interpret them as a guide. The significant elements in the dream are water, the bridge, and the forest: the dream as a source of creativity, the dream as a source of a connection to the soul and the unconscious. Maybe the soul and the forest represent your inner world. Super-realism is the method of feeling the things around you: you want to touch them and be close to them.

RITA: With super-realism, you can see all the details of things: you can see the patterns of a leaf or a snowflake enlarged and you can feel their textures without even touching them, such as the *talit* in the picture of the dream.

JAY: As I said before, the elements of this dream are very significant. The bridge is a symbol of the bridge to the soul that connects the unconscious. The water and forest are symbols of the inner world. Water is also a symbol of the soul. The fact that your perception of your surroundings is super-realistic, to visualize them, to imagine them, to expand upon them. You do this in order to escape the deterioration of life and perception that was your experience in the Holocaust. Becoming an artist was one of the potent fulfillments of your life; because creativity saved your life in the Holocaust, it gives you a channel of expression that helps you make order in your inner life and access greater consciousness.

RITA: Super-realism is a way of perceiving things acutely, so that it is possible to view each item's individual splendor. Especially in nature, everything has a special pattern, like a leaf, snowflake, or the cells in the human body. Super-realism is an art that is larger than life. The tiny details and inscriptions hold a lot of mystery for me, and produce in me an intense experience. I have never taken any drugs, but I know people who take drugs and have intense experiences perhaps similar to my experience of super-realism.

JAY: Freud said, "Dreams are the way to your soul. Dreams are the royal road to the unconscious." Your dreams demonstrate a desire to grasp your inner life. Your dreams are not chaotic. Unlike your conscious life, they have the authentic knowledge of your self. You need a spiritual guide, because there is so much material that is trying to come out, but it is stuck in your innards and creating stagnation.

RITA: That reminds me of a poem I wrote when I was studying art therapy for my MA in Boston. I called the poem "Muddy Waters."

MUDDY WATERS

Sitting by the pond, watching the butterflies and other creatures fly about. The water is stagnant and does not move, does not flow, not a ripple or a sound is heard anywhere except the occasional sound of a bird flying.

> Birches and weeds sitting in clumps, brownish muddiness.
> What can move this stickiness, I ask again and again.
> What can whirl it around, I ask again,
>   I ask what can move this
> Muddy pond into action, into life?

> For the trees, it is a mirror, for the bridge it is a shadow.
> What is it for me I ask again, I ask?
> I cannot move, not backwards nor forwards,
>   not to the left nor to the right, I cannot lift my weight.
> What will wake me from my slumber?
> I ask again, I ask.

> Lo and behold, something is moving, slowly steadily,
>   without hurry, without haste.
> Sliding through the Muddy Waters.
> A creature as ancient as the oceans, an image I met
>   in another world, another time, perhaps.
> It is bringing a message, is it bringing me hope?
> Will I, will I move out of the Stuckness, will I move
>   slowly and steadily like the turtle in the pond?

BIBLIOGRAPHY

Freud, Sigmund. *The Interpretation of Dreams.* New York: Avon Books, 1965.

Hillman, James. *The Dream and the Underworld.* New York: Harper and Row, 1979.

Jacobi, Jolande. *The Psychology of C.G. Jung.* New Haven and London: Yale University Press, 1973.

Johnson, Robert A. *Inner Work.* New York: HarperCollins Publishers, 1986.

Johnson, Robert A. *Owning Your Own Shadow.* New York: HarperCollins Publishers, 1986.

Jung, C.G. *The Collected Works of C.G. Jung.* Edited by Sir Herbert Read, Dr. Michael Fordham, Dr. Gerard Adler, and William McGuire. Translated by R.F.C. Hull. Bollingen Series xx. Princeton, NJ: Princeton University Press, 1970.

Kaczerginski, S. *Hurban Vilne* [The destruction of Vilna]. New York: Cyco-Bicher Farlag, 1947.

Katz, John. *Hayonah shekashlah* [The dove that failed]. Tel Aviv: Yaron Golan Publishing, 2006.

———. "Turmont between Poland and Lithuania, 1914–1945." Unpublished article, 2007.